Contents

Acknowledgements .... *i*

Foreword .... *ii*

About the Author -- Venerable Master Hsing Yun ..... *vi*

Introduction *1*

The Importance of the Four Noble Truths in Buddhism *7*

Parables Explicating the Four Noble Truths as Discoursed by the Buddha *23*

Development of the Mahayana's Four Universal Vows *51*

The Implementation from Four Nobel Truths to the Four Universal Vows *71*

Conclusion *105*

Endotes *110*

Acknowledgements

We received a lot of help from many people and we want to thank them for their efforts in making the publication of this book possible. We especially appreciate Venerable Tzu Jung, the Chief Executive of Fo Guang Shan International Translation Center (F.G.S.I.T.C.), Venerable Hui Chuan, the Abbot of Hsi Lai Temple, and Venerable Yi Chao, the Director of F.G.S.I.T.C. for their support and leadership; Ching Tay and Mu-Tzen Hsu for thier translation; Brenda Bolinger for her editing; Bill Maher, Echo Tsai, Oscar Mauricio for their proofreading; Audrey Her and Madelon wheeler - Gibb for their collecting datas; Mei-Chi Shih for her book and cover design; Venerable Miao Han and Mae Chu, for preparing the manuscript for publication. Our appreciation also goes to everyone who has supported this project from its conception to its completion.

Foreword

"*F*rom the Four Noble Truths to the Four Universal Vows" is the latest of Venerable Grand Master Hsing Yun's erudite writings in Chinese to be made available in a lucid, readable English translation. Its subtitle "An Integration of the Mahayana and Theravada Schools" illustrates the prime objective of the learned writer's on-going effort to harmonize the teachings and the practices of different schools of Buddhism. He stands out as the most influential reconciler and bridge-builder among schools, sects and traditions of Buddhism and his magnificent interpretation of Humanistic Buddhism is hailed as an effective umbrella concept to unify the Buddhist world for the application of the teachings of the Buddha for the well-being of humanity here and today.

This short treatise is a masterful presentation. The Grand Mater displays his deep and wide-ranging scholarship by drawing on a board spectrum of Buddhist literature spanning the Pali Canon of

Southern Buddhism, its counterpart in the Agama Sutras of the Chinese Tripitaka, the great Mahayana Sutras, and a variety of Sanskrit and Chinese treatises of specific Buddhist schools. Few scholars in the world can match the Grand Master's command of this vast literature or the facility with which he delves into them for appropriate quotes in support of his splendid appreciation of the relevance of Buddhism to life.

The Four Noble Truths, according to all Buddhist traditions, represent the very first formulation of Sakyamuni Buddha's world-view and path of salvation. As the Grand Master has stressed several times in this book, all teachings and practices of all schools of Buddhism emanate from the Four Noble Truths and are founded on them. He has rightly chosen this most fundamental of the Buddha's teachings to re-emphasize the harmony which prevails in all forms of Buddhism at the highest level of their doctrinal identity. Nothing establishes the unity of Buddhism more convincingly than the common acceptance of the Four Noble Truths as the fountainhead of all Buddhist doctrines. How effectively the Grand Master has demonstrated this truth by quoting from principal scriptures of every Buddhist tradition!

The Grand Master is an impeccable researcher. He has put together the various formulations of the Four Mahayana Vows according to different sutras and sastras. Here again, he demonstrates the commonality which pervades Buddhism.

He even proceeds to explain how in the Vajrayana tradition of Tibetan Buddhism the Four Vows were expanded to Five Vows, dividing the Fourth Vow into two as follows:

> Tathagatas are infinite, I vow to serve them.
> Buddhahood is supreme, I vow to obtain it.

The most admirable achievement of the Grand Master in this book is that he finds through the Four Universal Vows a practical basis for the practice of Buddhism in the contemporary world. He concludes that "in essence, the Buddha delivered his teachings through two distinctive methods: 'Teach relative to one's potential; and prescribe according to one's illness'". He proceeds to outline the four Reliances for learning the Dharma:

Rely on the Dharma, not on the instructor,
Rely on its meaning, not on the words,
Rely on wisdom, not on knowledge,
Rely on unconditioned dharmas, not on conditioned dharmas.

He equated learning with practice but would emphasize understanding and self-reliance. "In reality", the Grand Master tells us, "Buddhahood is not impossible to achieve! If, from understanding the Four Noble Truths to the fulfillment of the Four Universal Vows, we are able to inspire and make vows in accordance with the Dharma, practice diligently without indolence, and accumulate blessings, virtues, and good conditions, then Buddhahood is within our reach."

I have read this book with profit. It is a must for those who value Buddhism for its perennial applicability to life. It is a must for those who seek evidence of the remarkable unity within the diversity of Buddhism. It is a must for all who share in the Grand Master's lofty thoughts and timely guidance.

Ananda W.P. Guruge

Former Ambassador of Sri Lanka to UNESCO,
France and USA

Former Senior Special Advisor to the
Director-General of UNESCO

About Venerable Master Hsing Yun

Venerable Master Hsing Yun was born in Jiangdu, Jiangsu province, China, in 1927. Tonsured under Venerable Master Zhikai at age twelve, he became a novice monk at Qixia Vihara School and Jiaoshan Buddhist College. He was fully ordained in 1941, and is the 48th Patriarch of the Linji (Rinzai) Chan school.

He went to Taiwan in 1949 where he undertook to revitalizing Chinese Mahayana Buddhism on the island with a range of activities novel for its time. In 1967, he founded the Fo Guang Shan (Buddha's Light Mountain) Buddhist Order, and had since established more than a hundred temples in Taiwan and on every continent worldwide. Hsi Lai Temple, the United States Headquarters, was built outside Los Angeles in 1988.

At present , there are nearly two thousand

monks and nuns in the Fo Guang Shan Buddhist Order. The organization also oversees sixteen Buddhist colleges; four publishing houses including, Buddha's Light Publishing, Hsi Lai University Press; four universities, one of which is Hsi Lai University in Los Angeles; a secondary school; a satellite television station; an orphanage; and a nursing home for the elderly.

A prolific writer and an inspiring speaker, Master Hsing Yun has written many books on Buddhist sutras and a wide spectrum of topics over the past five decades. Most of his speeches and lectures were compiled into essays defining Humanistic Buddhism and outlining its practice. Some of his writings and lectures are translated into different languages such as English, Spanish, German, Russian, Japanese, Korean etc.

The Venerable Master is also the founder of Buddha's Light International Association, a worldwide organization of lay Buddhists dedicated to the propagation of Buddhism, with over 130 chapters and more than a million in membership.

From the Four Noble Truths

To the Four Universal Vows

-An Integration of the Mahayana and Theravada Schools

Introduction

The Four Noble Truths that the Buddha awakened to are the universal truth of suffering, the cause of suffering, the cessation of suffering, and the path leading to the cessation of suffering. From these Four Noble Truths, numerous Buddhist teachings were developed. Even so, on the basis of this universal truth, the Buddha intentionally developed and categorized these teachings into different levels of doctrines[1] for the benefit of Buddhist practitioners. Subsequently, through the integration with everyday life, the Four Universal Vows emerged. The following is a brief illustration of the association between the Four Universal Vows and the Four Noble Truths.

The truth of suffering refers to the suffering of sentient beings;[2] hence, the necessity of making the vow, "Sentient beings are infinite, I vow to liberate them."

The truth of the cause of suffering implicates

that suffering is the result of the accumulation of karma;[3] thus, the need for making the vow, "Afflictions are infinite, I vow to eradicate them."

The truth of the path leading to the cessation of suffering is to reinforce sentient beings to further practice the Path; hence, the importance of making the vow, "Dharmas[4] are inexhaustible, I vow to study them."

Lastly, the truth of the cessation of suffering marks the potential for every sentient being to attain Buddhahood; resulting in the vow, "Buddhahood is supreme, I vow to obtain it."

At the time when the Buddha became enlightened to the mundane and supramundane truths that are the Four Noble Truths, he was in deep contemplation and meditation under a bodhi tree. Later, he extensively discoursed on the Four Noble Truths to the world. The First Setting in Motion of the Wheel of the Dharma[5] is known as the "Three Turnings of the Dharma Wheel."[6] At his first discourse assem-

bly on the Four Noble Truths, called "Turning the Dharma Wheel for Recognition," the Buddha defined and explained the Four Noble Truths, which include:
Thus is suffering, which is oppressive,
Thus is the cause of suffering, which beckons;
Thus is the cessation of suffering, which is attainable,
Thus is the path, which is practicable.

His second assembly was called "Turning the Dharma Wheel for Encouragement," where he exhorted and guided his disciples to practice the Four Noble Truths in order to eradicate afflictions and accomplish liberation. The content included:
Thus is suffering, you should know,
Thus is the cause of suffering, you should end;
Thus is the cessation of suffering, you should actualize,
Thus is the path, you should practice.

In the Buddha's third assembly, called "Turning the Dharma Wheel for Realization," he told his disciples that he had realized the Four Noble Truths, and that they, too possessed the potential to actualize the Four Noble Truths if they practiced diligently.

Included in the content were:
Thus is suffering, I have known,
Thus is the cause of suffering, I have eradicated;
Thus is the cessation of suffering, I have actualized,
Thus is the path, I have practiced.

From the aforementioned, it can be suggested that the first two Noble Truths are the cause and effect in the mundane world. While the cause of suffering is the origin, suffering is the result. The same is applied to the last two Noble Truths as the cause and effect in the supramundane world. While the path is the cause, the cessation of suffering is the effect.

The Four Noble Truths may be a common topic of discussion among Buddhists. However, to fulfill them, we must proceed through the "way of vowing"[7] of the Four Universal Vows prior to the "way of practicing,"[8] with the latter consisting of the six perfections[9] that embody the bodhisattva path. It short, it can also be deduced that the Four Universal Vows of Mahayana Buddhism are the developments of practice based on the teachings of the Four Noble Truths originally discoursed by the Buddha. This is also a process through which Buddhism has been able to become a multi-faceted religion.[10]

From the dharmas of the Four Noble Truths to the actualization of the Four Universal Vows, it is also evident that the Buddha's teachings are characterized by a sense of contemporariness, continuity, and progress. His teachings are systematically interconnected, and therefore, have enabled the Dharma to withstand through history, time, and space. Furthermore, contrary to the belief of many that the Mahayana and Theravada are of separate teachings, they are in fact very much integrated, of one and not two. Thus, it is the primary objective of this paper to demonstrate the existence of this integration.

The Importance of the Four Noble Truths in Buddhism

The Four Noble Truths are the fundamentals of all Buddhist teachings. When the Buddha attained enlightenment under the bodhi tree, he awoke to the truth of Dependent Origination.[11] However, the Buddha was concerned that if all of a sudden he discoursed on this truth, those who did not believe in Buddhism would be discouraged to learn it due to the profundity of this truth. As a result, at the first turning of the Dharma Wheel, the Buddha intentionally employed the Four Noble Truths to explain the theory of Dependent Origination between the cycle of birth and death[12] and the path of liberation. It was the Buddha's intention to inspire sentient beings with the determination to practice the path and to be free from suffering. This was the purpose for teaching sentient beings, "Know suffering, end the cause of suffering, practice the path, and attain the cessation of suffering."

Apart from the period of the First Setting in Motion of the Wheel of the Dharma, the Buddha also spoke on the Four Noble Truths before his parinirvana,[13] saying to his disciples, "Those of you who are still unclear on the Four Noble Truths, you may ask me quickly now. Seek certitude; do not hold on to doubts." The Buddha inquired three times in this manner, yet none of his disciples raised a question but for one. Aniruddha,[14] recognizing the Buddha's intention, repeated the Buddha's words and said, "While the sun can turn cold and the moon hot, the Four Noble Truths spoken by the Buddha will eternally remain unchanged" (*Sutra of the Teachings Bequeathed by the Buddha*).[15]

The Buddha's repeated emphasis on the Four Noble Truths demonstrates that they were expounded from beginning to end, their meanings never altered. This emphasis was illustrated during the First Setting in Motion of the Wheel of the Dharma when the Buddha discoursed three times on the wonderful meanings of the Four Noble Truths. It was also known as the "Three Turnings of the Dharma Wheel and the Twelve Aspects of the Four Noble Truths."[16]

The philosophy underlying the Four Noble Truths is comparable to the course of an illness. Suffering is likened to being ill, with the cause of suffering as the cause of illness, the path leading to the cessation of suffering as the prescribed medication for the illness, and finally, the cessation of suffering as the state of complete recovery from the illness (*Yogacarabhumi Sastra*).[17] In other words, the purpose of practicing Buddhism is to be free from all afflictions caused by greed, hatred, and ignorance, and ultimately attain the state of nirvana. Therefore, the Four Noble Truths will lead us from the state of confusion to the state of awakening; from the bondage of suffering and the cause of suffering to the freedom of the path leading to the cessation of suffering and the cessation of suffering. The *Commentary on the Madhyamika Sastra*[18] states, "The Four Noble Truths are the pivoting point of both confusion and awakening. If you are confused about them, chaos reigns within the six realms.[19] If you awaken to them, you ascend to the stage of the three vehicles."[20]

The Four Noble Truths also explicate the relationship between life and the cosmos, i.e. the cosmos where human beings reside, known as the mundane world, is composed of suffering and the cause of suffering. Consequently, to reach the supramundane Dharma realm where suffering and the cause of suffering are transcended, it is necessary to first learn the path leading to the cessation of suffering before cessation of suffering can be achieved.

In essence, the Four Noble Truths, the Twelve Links of Dependent Origination, and the Three Dharma Seals[21] are the basis of all Buddhist teachings. Although each doctrine has its own distinctive name, they share a common philosophy. The principles of the Twelve Links of Dependent Origination are the foundation of the Three Dharma Seals, while the Four Noble Truths are the embodiment of the Twelve Links of Dependent Origination. Furthermore, the commentaries of sutras developed later are all based on them. Therefore, they are called the fundamental doctrines of Buddhism.

The Buddha's emphasis on the importance of the Four Noble Truths is also noticed in many other sutras. For instance, in the *Gradual Discourses of the Buddha* (*Ekottarikagama*, fas. 36),[22] the Buddha exhorts, "Now [I] discourse the 'eight adversities,'[23] which are the important points of [my] teachings. [Confronting any] one adversity is as unfortunate as a piece of wood floating in the open sea [without direction]." Although [we] should be away from [any] one adversity, we still have the opportunity to learn the Dharma [in the future]. But if [we] are away from any one of the Four Noble Truths, we will be apart from the right path[24] forever."

Also in the *Connected Discourses of the Buddha* (*Samyuktagama*, fas.16),[25] the Buddha tells his disciples, "It is like someone throwing a cane into the air. When it falls back onto earth, either its end tip, middle section, or its grip will have first contact with the ground. For those sramana[26] or brahmans[27] who do not truly understand the truth of suffering, the truth of the cause of suffering, the truth of the cessation of suffering, and the truth of the path leading to the cessation of suffering, [you] should know that they would fall into the realm of hell, animal, or hungry ghost. Therefore, bhiksus,[28] if your clarity concerning the Four Noble Truths has not reached uninterrupted continuity, you should, by all means, investigate them diligently without abeyance."

The Buddha then continued speaking to the bhiksus, "The number of sentient beings who truly understand the truth of suffering, the truth of the cause of suffering, the truth of the cessation of suffering, and the truth of the path leading to the cessation of suffering, are equivalent to the amount of sand and stones in my hand. The number of those who have not truly understood the truth of suffering, the truth of the cause of suffering, the truth of the cessation of suffering, and the truth of the path leading to the cessation of suffering, are equivalent to the amount of sands and stones of the Himalayas. That number is incalculable. Therefore, bhiksus, if your understanding of the Four Noble Truths has not reached uninterrupted continuity, you should, by all means, give rise to the aspiration to advance and investigate them diligently without abeyance."

The Buddha also employed many parables to explain the importance of the Four Noble Truths. The *Connected Discourses of the Buddha*, fas. 15 records that when the Buddha discoursed at Deer Park,[29] he expounded that the world without the Four Noble Truths is a world in total darkness as though the sun is in hiding and the moon vanished. With the Four Noble Truths, the world is bathed with a magnificent brightness. The Buddha also told the bhiksus that those who did not truly understand the Four Noble Truths were easily influenced by external circumstances, and could not be their own masters, like cotton wool drifting in the wind without direction. Therefore, the Four Noble Truths need be truly learnt, understood, practiced, and attained. In the *Medallion Sutra on the Bodhisattva Path*,[30] the Buddha analogized a torch to the ability of the Four Noble Truths to penetrate ignorance, the first link of the Twelve Links of Dependent Origination. With frequent insight into the impermanence of all phenomena, we can be free from the entanglements of afflictions.

Moreover, the Buddha states in the *Four Part Vinaya* (*Dharmagupta Vinaya*, fas. 32),[31] "If I had not fulfilled the Four Noble Truths, the Three Turnings of the Dharma Wheel, and the Twelve Aspects, or if I had not truly understood the Four Noble Truths, I would not have accomplished the unexcelled path of Truth." The Buddha attained Buddhahood as a result of his enlightenment to complete understanding of the Four Noble Truths. Therefore, he told his disciples, "On the Four Noble Truths, the Three Turnings of the Dharma Wheel, and the Twelve Aspects, I have completely understood, today I have accomplished the unexcelled path of Truth" (*Four Part Vinaya*, fas. 32). "The meanings, the dharmas, and the cultivation of purification [of the Four Noble Truths] are beneficial and helpful in the pursuit of perfect wisdom, perfect awareness, and toward nirvana" (*Connected Discourses of the Buddha*, fas. 16). From the above, it can be deduced that if not for the presence of the Four Noble Truths in this universe, Sakyamuni Buddha would not have taught the Truth; and as such, there would be no

Dharma to be learnt, nor would the Sangha have existed.

Conclusively, the Four Noble Truths undoubtedly hold the highest and most prominent position among the Buddha's teachings. It is as described in the *Middle Length Discourses of the Buddha* (*Madhyamagama*, fas. 30),[32] "[In] the boundless wholesome Dharma, all other teachings are contained within the Four Noble Truths. In terms of the relations between the Four Noble Truths and others, the Four Noble Truths are the most supreme." Since the Four Noble Truths encapsulate the Buddhist teachings, below are four attributes of the Four Noble Truths:

(1) The Four Noble Truths are Buddhism

All dharmas in the mundane and supramundane realms arose from the Truth. For instance, it is a reality that life is suffering. Even when there is happiness in life, it is subjected to the suffering of impermanence.[33] This is an inescapable truth. Life's affliction as a result of the accumulation of karma is also a truth. Therefore, regardless if one is in the heavenly realm or the human world, a sage or a saint, one's existence remains abided by the Law of Dependent Origination, due to the accumulation of karma. There is no phenomenon in the universe that is exempt from the Law of Dependent Origination due to cause and effect. This law clearly explains all relationships in life. The above teaching on Dependent Origination due to cause and effect and the accumulation of karma, is a unique characteristic of Buddhism.

Although suffering and the cause of suffering are the cause and effect of our worldly existence, it need not be terrifying. This is because the latter two Noble Truths, the cessation of suffering and the path leading to the cessation of suffering, would lead us to transcend suffering and its cause. For instance, practicing the Eightfold Noble Path[34] can eliminate suffering and the cause of suffering, and direct us towards nirvana.

Therefore, while worldly truth teaches that every party can have a claim to be right, Buddhist truth is universal, inevitable, equal, and timeless. For example, Buddhism teaches that all phenomena are impermanent. Impermanence itself has the qualities of universality, inevitability, equality, and timelessness. Other basic doctrines such as emptiness, Dependent Origination, karma, and the Law of Cause and Effect, are also in accord with these principles. Notably, the Four Noble Truths possess these qualities and thus, will remain unchanged in any circumstance. They are the guiding principle for all phenomena. Furthermore, all teachings described in the sutras and sastras are submitted to the principle of the Four Noble Truths.

(2) The Four Noble Truths are the Buddhist sacred scriptures

Buddhism has numerous scriptures. The *Chinese Buddhist Canon*[35] contains sections such as the *Agamas, Lotus Sutra (Saddharmapundarika Sutra), Jatakas, Group of Discourses (Sutta Nipata), Yogacara, Mahasamnipata, Group of Sastras, Mahasamghata, Collection of Great Treasures (Maharatnakuta), Madhyamika, Vinaya, Prajna*, etc.

Regardless if it is a sutra or sastra, all are deeply rooted in the Four Noble Truths. Therefore, the Four Noble Truths are the fundamental teachings of early Buddhism. Even in later Buddhism, the development of the "three studies"—precepts, concentration, and wisdom; as well as the *Tripitaka*[36]—sutras, vinayas, and sastras, also arose from the Four Noble Truths.

It is stated in the *Treatise on the Middle Path* (*Mulamadhyamaka Karika*),[37] "If all phenomena in the world are non-existent, then there would not be formation and cessation. Without formation and cessation, there would not be the Four Noble Truths. Why? The arising of suffering comes from the cause of suffering. The cause of suffering is the root, and suffering is the effect. The elimination of suffering as well as the cause of suffering is thus called the cessation of suffering. That which leads to the cessation of suffering is called the path. The path is the cause; the cessation of suffering is the effect. Therefore, the Four Noble Truths have their own causes and effects. If there is no formation and cessation, there would not be the Four Noble Truths. Without the Four

Noble Truths, it is impossible to realize suffering, to eliminate the cause of suffering, to actualize the cessation of suffering, and to cultivate the path. ...Also, without the Four Noble Truths, the treasure of the Dharma would not exist."

Therefore, despite the numerous schools of doctrine in Buddhism, none are removed from the Four Noble Truths. In conclusion, the Four Noble Truths are not only considered the most important scripture but also the earliest scripture. For without the Four Noble Truths, all dharmas would not have existed.

(3) The Four Noble Truths are the framework of Buddhist teachings

While Confucianism[38] structures its teachings based on the "four ethical principles,"[39] the "eight cardinal values,"[40] the "three bonds in human relationships,"[41] and the "five constant virtues;"[42] Buddhism structures its teaching on the Four Noble Truths. Today, every school of Buddhism, including Mahayana, Theravada, and Vajrayana,[43] relies on the

Four Noble Truths as its framework. Moreover, the teachings in the *Tripitaka* and the twelve sections of the *Buddhist Canon*[44] are also based on the Four Noble Truths. Therefore, as long as we understand the Four Noble Truths, speak on the Four Noble Truths, and practice the Four Noble Truths, we can be said to have understood Buddhism. Nowadays, new learners of Buddhism should begin their practice by studying the Four Noble Truths. If one can comprehend the Four Noble Truths, one has understood the basis of Buddhism. Thereafter, it will not be difficult to approach the study of other components in Buddhism.

The Buddha spoke about the Four Noble Truths in many Dharma assemblies, repeatedly teaching the important relationship between the Four Noble Truths and life. There was one occasion when a splinter pierced the Buddha's toe and King Ajatasatru[45] was greatly concerned about the injury. To assuage the anxiety of everyone present at the assembly, the Buddha spoke on the Four Noble Truths.

(4) The Four Noble Truths are the hallmark of Buddhism

Every country has its national flag and every school or society has its logo. While Christianity has the cross as its symbol, Buddhism has the Dharma Wheel, which originated when the Buddha initiated the "Three Turnings of the Dharma Wheel" to deliver the Four Noble Truths. On the other hand, Buddhism nowadays also has its own flag, called the five-color flag. It symbolizes the sharing of the same basic doctrines of the five vehicles,[46] with the Four Noble Truths as its fundamental center.

Although India is Buddhism's country of origin, it has since been introduced to various places throughout the world. Having taken root in many foreign lands, Buddhism has adapted into new forms according to the respective local culture, language, and custom. Furthermore, despite the variation in interpretation about the Buddha and the Buddhist doctrines among Buddhists from different areas, there has always been a consensus about using both the Dharma Wheel and the Four Noble Truths as the hallmarks of Buddhism.

There are people who criticize Buddhist communities for being too fragmented and diverse. Often times, different sects of Buddhists express different perspectives that are sometimes contradictive to the original teachings. If we hope to unite Buddhism, we should practice the "Three Turnings of the Dharma Wheel" through the study of the Four Noble Truths.

Parables Explicating the Four Noble Truths as Discoursed by the Buddha

As previously stated, the Buddha spoke the Four Noble Truths to the five bhiksus[47] in Deer Park soon after he attained enlightenment. This teaching remains the fundamental doctrine of Theravada, Mahayana, and Vajrayana Buddhism, and is considered the only means to liberation within the worldly and transcendental existence. Later Buddhists considered the Four Noble Truths as the practice of the sravakas and the pratyeka-buddhas[48] and demeaned it as the teaching of the "Small Vehicle."[49] However, many Mahayana sutras, including the *Lion's Roar of Queen Srimala Sutra* (*Srimaladevisimhanada*)[50] and the *Great Nirvana Sutra* (*Mahaparinirvana*),[51] not only interpret the Four Noble Truths from the Mahayana perspective but have also further expanded its meanings.

In the *Gradual Discourses of the Buddha*, the

Buddha discoursed the Four Noble Truths as the following, "The so-called 'truth of suffering' relates to the suffering of birth, aging, illness, and death; the suffering of affliction, sorrow, and grief; the suffering from association with the unloved; the suffering of separation from the loved; and the suffering of unfulfilled desire. In short, the truth of suffering is a result of the 'five aggregates.'[52] ...The so-called 'truth of the cause of suffering' is the inter-relatedness of craving and desire, which constantly contaminates the mind. ...The so-called 'truth of the cessation of suffering' is the complete extinction of craving and desire that will never return. ...The so-called 'truth of the path leading to the cessation of suffering' is the Eightfold Noble Path, which includes right view, right thought, right speech, right action, right livelihood, right effort, right mindfulness, and right concentration."

The truths as stated in the Four Noble Truths are a reality. Buddhism uses the Four Noble Truths to explain the phenomena of the universe. Suffering and the cause of suffering represent the cause and effect in the mundane world. In contrast, the cessation of suffering and the path leading to the cessation of suffering represent the cause and effect in the supramundane world. While suffering is the effect in the mundane world, the cause of suffering is the root. Comparatively, in the supramundane world, the cessation of suffering is the effect, and the path leading to the cessation of suffering is the root.

Therefore, in accordance with the Law of Cause and Effect,[53] the sequence of the Four Noble Truths should be listed as the cause of suffering, suffering, the path leading to the cessation of suffering, and the cessation of suffering. Why would the Buddha speak first about the effects before the cause? This is because sentient beings have the predisposition to comprehend effects but not their cause. In order to guide and transform sentient beings, the Buddha first had to clearly demonstrate suffering. This in turn motivates sentient beings to remove themselves from suffering. Secondly, by demonstrating the cause of suffering, sentient beings will be inspired to eliminate the cause of suffering. Thirdly, through the display of the blissful state of nirvana, the Buddha instigates the aspiration of sentient beings. Finally, by accounting the path, it allows sentient beings to practice and uphold it.

According to the *Agama Sutras*, the *Abhidharmamahavibhasa Sastra*,[54] and the *Mahayanabhidharma Samuccaya Vyakhya*,[55] the meanings within the Four Noble Truths are as follows:

(1) The truth of suffering

In general, suffering is the state when the body and mind are driven by afflictions. The truth of suffering elucidates that transmigration is suffering and that life itself is suffering. According to the sutras, suffering can be categorized into two, three, four, eight, eighty-four thousand, and countless numbers of sufferings. In modern terms, suffering can be divided into the following categories, the disharmony of personal relationships (e.g. the suffering of separation from loved ones and association with unloved ones); the disharmony of the physical condition (e.g. the suffering of aging, illness, and death); the disharmony of mental states (e.g. the suffering of greed, anger, and ignorance); the disharmony of material comforts (e.g. the suffering of crowded living space and unfulfilled desires); the disharmony of affairs (e.g. the suffering of unemployment and failing an examination); the disharmony of society (e.g. the suffering of excessive crime and economic recession); the disharmony of nature (e.g. the suffering of an inability to acclimatize to hot and cold weather); the disharmony of external conditions (e.g. the suffering of compliment, scorn, slander, degeneration, pain, and joy).

Regardless of the types of suffering that exist in the world, the reason Buddhism teaches suffering is to enable us to understand the truth of suffering and lead us to eliminate suffering. In other words, realizing the existence of suffering is only a part of the process. The ultimate purpose of teaching the truth of suffering in Buddhism is to enable the elimination of suffering and subsequently the attainment of liberation.

(2) The truth of the cause of suffering

The cause of suffering refers to the origin of suffering. The term "origin" represents the accumulation and attraction of karma. According to the *Treatise on the Demonstration of Mind-Only (Vijnaptimatratasiddhi Sastra)*,[56] "Birth and death succeed each other. As a result of delusion, karmic effect ensues, which is naturally followed by suffering." Sentient beings are driven by affliction, which in turn is the result of ignorance, craving, desire, hatred, etc. Afflictions subsequently trigger and accumulate abundant negative karma, resulting in various effects of suffering. The endless cycle of birth and death exists due to the presence of a never-ending chain of afflictions, karma, and effect of suffering. In short, affliction can ignite karma, which nurtures the continuance of the cycle of birth and death.

Afflictions can be recognized by several terms. Afflictions, which obstruct our intrinsic nature, are called "obstructions" or "shrouding." Afflictions are also likened to ropes that are coiled and twisted around our mind; hence, are known as "knots" or "entanglements." They are also referred as "binding" or "restraints" because they can constrain the bodies and minds of sentient beings. Since they can pollute the nature of sentient beings, they are called "filth." Afflictions are also known as "gushing current" because they are like a flood that can erode good attributes. They are described as "driving force" because sentient beings are driven by them in the cycle of birth and death. Afflictions are named "yoke" because they prevent sentient beings from escaping the cycle of birth and death. Afflictions are like a thick jungle and thus, are called "dense forest." Afflictions that are buried deep within the consciousness disturb the harmony within the body and mind in a very subtle manner, even during our sleep. Thus, they are called "that which accompanies sleep." Afflictions are also like dusts that can taint the mind and so are called "scattering dusts."

From the above, it is clear that afflictions are not inherent. They arise because of our temporary delusion and, therefore, they are described as "momentary dusts." In addition to the terms mentioned so far, Buddhism uses other metaphors including fire, poisonous arrows, tigers and wolves, and dangerous pitfalls to connote afflictions.

In order to be free from afflictions, we have to eliminate the cause that triggers them and never create further negative karma. This is like the saying, "Eliminating old karma in the midst of responding to the conditions; never planting new seedlings." Should we achieve this, a blissful life is not far away. Therefore, a thorough understanding of the cause of suffering is a necessary step before we can arrive at the extinction of suffering.

(3) The cessation of suffering

Cessation of suffering means the elimination of afflictions of greed, hatred, and ignorance, which subsequently gives rise to the nature of "suchness." This is equivalent to nirvana. In the *Explanation of the Mahayana* (fas.18),[57] and the *Great Commentary on the Flower Ornament Sutra* (fas. 52),[58] "Nirvana is a Sanskrit term for 'the cessation of suffering.'"

Nirvana is the liberation that truth seekers actualize through practicing the Path, after having understood the truth of suffering and removed the cause of suffering. It is a state that transcends afflictions and suffering, self and others, right and wrong, discrimination, obstructions, and ignorance. In other words, it is a state of oneness, freedom, completion, and lastly, transcendence from birth and death.

Nirvana is a state that can be further detailed as:
i) Without birth. Nirvana has no birth and death, nor change and discrimination. It is a state without formation and extinction. In this ultimate state, neither afflictions nor tranquility, contamination nor clarity, the external nor self exists any longer.
ii) Without an abode. When one attains nirvana, one actualizes *dharmakaya*,[59] which permeates everywhere. Therefore, one who is in nirvana will never be confined to any abode.
iii) Without a "self." The state of nirvana breaks our attachment to "self," and allows us to achieve the true freedom of "non-self." From "non-self," we establish a "true self." This is referred to by the saying, "Love

without attachment is true love, a 'self' without 'self' is the 'true self.'" The self that we will discover upon nirvana is the "true self."

iv) Without attaining. Nirvana is the spiritual land of bliss. It is composed of Dharma joy, tranquility, supreme joy, eternal happiness, completion of blessings and wisdom, liberation, "true self," and the ultimate reality. These are the result of attainment without attaining, and emptiness without existence.

The bliss of nirvana can be attained by everyone in every moment. It is the ultimate ideal state after all suffering and causes of suffering have been eliminated. If we can realize and eliminate the origins of suffering, i.e., desire and craving, we would naturally enter the state of nirvana.

(4) The path leading to the cessation of suffering

The path means "that which leads to the arrival at nirvana." The path is the process that can lead us from the shore of suffering to the shore of nirvana. In general, it is known as the Eightfold Noble Path; the teaching that the Buddha taught during the

First Setting in Motion of the Wheel of the Dharma. The Eightfold Noble Path is:

i) Right View. This includes correct understanding of the Law of Cause and Effect, wholesome and unwholesome karma; the awareness that all phenomena are empty in their true nature and, thus are impermanent, and that form and emptiness are not dual.

ii) Right Thought. This includes correct perception that our bodies will eventually decay, sensations cause suffering, thoughts are momentary and impermanent, and that the nature of all phenomena is without a "self."

iii) Right Speech. This includes using the correct language to speak true words, compassionate words, complimenting words, and beneficial words.

iv) Right Action. This includes correct conduct in refraining from killing, stealing, sexual misconduct, and intoxication.

v) Right Livelihood. This includes correct living of a reasonable economic life, an altruistic life, a harmonious communal life, and an unadulterated life.

vi) Right Effort. This includes correct diligence in

developing wholesomeness that has not arisen, increasing wholesomeness that has arisen, preventing the arising of unwholesomeness, and eliminating unwholesomeness that has arisen.

vii) Right Mindfulness. This includes correct determination in one's belief, non-attachment to phenomena, misconception of the Law of Cause and Effect, and not giving rise to the confusion of birth and death.

viii) Right Concentration. This includes the *samadhi*[60] attained through meditating on the five contemplations,[61] the six wondrous ways to nirvana,[62] the harmony of body, speech, and mind, and the nine stages of meditative concentration.[63]

In conclusion, the first Noble Truth when perceived with wisdom connotes that the world is like a house on fire, i.e., filled with the pains of suffering. The second Noble Truth when perceived with wisdom indicates that afflictions and the creation of karma are the roots of the suffering from the cycle of birth and death. The third Noble Truth signifies that from wisdom, one must attain one's true nature and achieve ultimate nirvana to escape from the cycle of birth and death. Finally, the fourth Noble Truth is the process leading to ultimate nirvana.

In the *Flower Ornament Sutra* (*Avamtasaka Sutra*),[64] the Buddha described the names that the Four Noble Truths are known as in the various worlds. Following are the names as described by the Buddha known in each respective world.

(1) The Saha World:[65]

The truth of suffering – wrongdoing, oppression, changing, grasping, gathering, torns, dependence on the sense organs, falsity, carbuncle, ignorant conduct.

The truth of the cause of suffering – binding, decay and extinction, desire, deluded thoughts, greediness, decision, net, erroneous speech, following along, awry faculties.

The truth of the cessation of suffering – non-contention, liberation from defilement, tranquility, formlessness, deathlessness, absence of self-nature, without hindrance, extinction, suchness, abiding in true nature.

The truth of the path leading to the cessation of suffering – one vehicle, proceed towards tranquility, leading, ultimately without discrimination, equality, putting down burdens, having no object of desire, following the Noble Truth, the practice of the divine, ten treasuries.

(2) The Esoteric Teaching World:
The truth of suffering – the sense of seeking, not being liberated, the basis of binding, doing what should not be done, contending in all kinds of situations, without the capability to analyze, being relied on, extreme suffering, and hyperactivity.

The truth of the cause of suffering – following the stream of birth and death, habitual attachment, in flame, continuing in cycles, defiled senses, continuing existence of karma, unwholesome deeds, grasping, the causes of illness, and categorization.

The truth of the cessation of suffering – the supreme truth, liberated, praiseworthy, peace, a good place to enter, taming, faultlessness, departing from greed, determined decision.

The truth of the path leading to the cessation of suffering – brave general supreme practice, transcending, with skillful means, the eye of equality, detached from extremes, awakening, embracing, the supreme eye, and contemplating the truth.

(3) The Supreme World
The truth of suffering – fear, individual mortality, despicable, what should be worked on, changes, that which provokes resentment, deceptive usurper, hard to collaborate with, false discrimination, and powerful.

The truth of the cause of suffering – decadent, ignorance, great rancor, sharp knife, flavor of destruction, spiteful, not one's own belongings, harmful guidance, increasing darkness, and destroying goodness.

The truth of the cessation of suffering – significant meaning, benefit, the supreme goals, limitless, what should be seen, free from of discrimination, supreme taming, constant equality, worthy of living with, and unconditional.

The truth of the path leading to the cessation of suffering – able to turn, the highest rank, determined decision, unbreakable, skillful means, liberation, not inferior or bad, without obstruction, essence of liberation, and capable of liberating.

(4) The Undefiled World:
The truth of suffering – remorse, dependency, cyclical, reside within walls, one flavor, false doctrine, dwelling at home, a place of deluded attachments, deluded perception, and incalculable.

The truth of the cause of suffering – what is not substantial, meaningless words, not pure, place of arising, grasping, lowness, increasing, heavy burdens, that can give rise, coarseness.

The truth of the cessation of suffering – the

unexcelled, complete elimination, undefiled, unexcelled faculties, independence, elimination of confusion, the most supreme, the ultimate, and breaking the seal.

The truth of the path leading to the cessation of suffering – unbreakable, portion of skillful means, the basis of liberation, the reality of intrinsic nature, unblameable, the boundary of all existences, the most pristine, and pristine insight.

(5) The Abundance World:
The truth of suffering – the place of craving and grasping, the root of danger and harm, accomplished through accumulation, discriminating faculties, increase, formation and extinction, obstruction, the blades of knives and swords.

The truth of the cause of suffering - despicable, limitless, unlovable, coarseness, craving and grasping, vessel, and motioning.

The truth of the cessation of suffering – ends

the continuity, revelation, no description, nothing to cultivate, no object to be seen, nothing to work on, nirvana, completely burnt out, putting down the heavy burden, and cleansed.

The truth of the path leading to the cessation of suffering – the practice leading to nirvana, the practice of liberating, diligent practice and experience, going to peace, infinite life, comprehensive understanding, the ultimate path, difficult to practice, and arriving to the other shore.

(6) The All-embracing World
The truth of suffering – able to usurp, not good friends, full of fear, erroneous speech, the nature of hell, untruth, the burden of greed, roots of deep gravity, changing with feelings, ultimately empty.

The truth of the cause of suffering – greediness, false discrimination, wrongdoing, hasty recklessness, able to grasp and attach, perceptions, bears results, indescribable, inapprehensible, and transmigrating.

The truth of cessation of suffering – non-regression, beyond words, formlessness, delightful, solid, supremely wondrous, free from ignorance, extinction, dissociation from unwholesomeness, and transcending.

The truth of the path of leading to the cessation of suffering – beyond speech, non-contention, instruction, transfer of merits, great skillful means, variety of skills, space-like, the practice of tranquility, and full comprehension of the supramundane truth.

(7) The Beneficial World:
The truth of suffering – heavy burden, unsteadiness, like a thief, aging and death, produced by desire, transmigration, exhaustion, unwholesome state, growth, a sharp knife.

The truth of the cause of suffering – decadence, murky, regression, weakness, loss, opposing, disharmony, doing, grasping, and wishing.

The truth of the cessation of suffering – free from imprisonment, reality, free from suffering, protection, free from unwholesomeness, following along, foundation, abandoning the causes, unconditional, and non-continuous.

The truth of the path leading to the cessation of suffering – beyond all existences, the seal of totality, the treasury of samadhi, obtaining light, the teaching of non-regression, eliminating all outflows, the great spacious way, ability to tame, having peace, and the root of non-transmigration.

(8) The Rarefied World:
The truth of suffering – risky desires, place of bondage, unwholesome action, sensations, without shame, rooted in greed, constant disintegration, the characteristic of fire, full of agitation and anxiety.

The truth of the cause of suffering – spacious ground, inclination, distanced from wisdom, retains troubles, fear, laxity, collecting, attachment, master of the house, and continuous binding.

The truth of the cessation of suffering – fulfillment, immortality, non-self, without self-nature, the end of discrimination, dwelling in peace and joy, limitless, severing transmigration, severing compulsive mental activity, and non-duality.

The truth of the path leading to the cessation of suffering – great brightness, ocean of elucidation, examining meaning, the way of harmony, free from grasping and attachment, severing the continuity, great spacious way, basis of equality, skillful means, and supreme insight.

(9) The Joy World:
The truth of suffering – transmigration, birth, habitual attachment, heavy burden, discrimination, an unwholesome abode, and the characteristic of affliction.

The truth of the cause of suffering – ground, conveniences, inappropriate timing, untrue dharma, bottomless, collecting, departing from precepts, afflictions, narrow and inferior perspective, and gathering of defilement.

The truth of the cessation of suffering – breaking off dependency, non-indulging, reality, equality, purity, without illness, non-false, formlessness, free and easy, and birthless.

The truth of the path leading to the cessation of suffering – entering into the unexcelled realm, severing the cause of suffering, transcending comparativeness, spacious nature, the end of discrimination, the path of transcendental power, various skillful means, the practice of right thought, the road of continuous tranquility, and leading to liberation.

(10) The Door Lock World

The truth of suffering – form of decadence, like a broken vessel, product of ego, tendency toward the six realms, numerous transmigrations, door of various unwholesomeness, essence of suffering, can be abandoned, and tastelessness.

The truth of the cause of suffering – action, the poison of anger, coming together, sensation, self-centered, multiple poison, false name, opposing, affliction, and horrifying.

The truth of the cessation of suffering – no accumulation, ungraspable, wonderful medicine, indestructible, non-attachment, immeasurable, spaciousness, awakening, free from contamination, and no obstruction.

The truth of the path leading to the cessation of suffering – the practice of peace, free from desire, the ultimate reality, entering into truth, nature of ultimacy, manifestation of purity, concentration, leading to liberation, deliverance, and supreme conduct.

(11) The Trembling Sound World
The truth of suffering – the worldly, arrogance, the characteristic of habitual attachment, torrent, unenjoyable, hidden, that which vanishes swiftly, and hard to tame.

The truth of the cause of suffering – should be tamed, tendency of the mind, binding, arising with every thought, combination, discrimination, and drifting along.

The truth of the cessation of suffering – no reliance, ungraspable, returning, free from contention, good and pure, limitless, spaciousness, and invaluable.

The truth of the path leading to the cessation of suffering – able to defeat the foes, the seal of understanding, able to enter the true nature, undefiable, infinite meanings, entry into wisdom, the way of harmony, everlasting stability, and supreme truth.
(*Flower Ornament Sutra*, ch.8. English reference from *The Flower Ornament Scripture* by Thomas Cleary.)

To enable his disciples to accept the teachings with ease, the Buddha often used parables when discoursing the Dharma, except for during the "Three Turnings of the Dharma Wheel." The importance of parables in Buddhism is undeniable. For example, the *Lotus Sutra's Parable of Medicinal Herbs* and the *Parable of the Impoverished Men* are considered to be among the most beautiful Buddhist literature. Even among the twelve sections of the *Buddhist*

Canon, one is dedicated as the section of *Parables*.

In discoursing the Four Noble Truths, the Buddha also used many parables to illustrate the teachings. For instance, in the *Collection of Great Treasures* (*Maharatnakuta*),[66] the Buddha expounds the truth of suffering as "a resented thief, a carbuncle, an arrow, imprisonment, a broken arrow, not free and easy, and non-self." In the *Treatise on the Four Noble Truths* (*Catuhsatya-nirdesha*),[67] the Buddha employed the following parables:

i) Suffering is like a disease,
The cause of suffering is like the cause of the disease,
The cessation of suffering is like being free of the disease,
And the path leading to the cessation of suffering is like the medicinal cure for the disease.
ii) Suffering is like a fire,
The cause of suffering is like the firewood,
The cessation of suffering is like the extinguishment of the fire,
And the path leading to the cessation of suffering is like the basis for extinguishing the fire.

iii) Resentment is called suffering,
To incur hatred is called the cause of suffering,
To eliminate hatred is called the cessation of suffering,
And the basis of elimination is called the path leading to the cessation of suffering.
iv) Clothing is called suffering,
Dust is called the cause of suffering,
Dustlessness is called the cessation of suffering,
And the basis of dustlessness is called the path leading to the cessation of suffering.
v) Suffering is like being in debt,
The cause of suffering is like being in poverty,
The cessation of suffering is like being free from poverty,
The path leading to the cessation of suffering is like being wealthy.
vi) Suffering is like being burned,
The cause of suffering is like the wick,
The cessation of suffering is like being refreshed,
The path leading to the cessation of suffering is like the means to refreshment.
vii) Suffering is like the effect of poisoning,
The cause of suffering is like the poison,
The cessation of suffering is like being free from the poison,

The path leading to the cessation of suffering is like the antidote.

Apart from the above, the Buddha also observed, "While ordinary people in the mundane world are tormented by the [five] aggregates (*skandhas*), they remain attached to them. It is like a dependency on the enemy, perceiving them as relatives and friends. This dependency and attachment to the aggregates are the causes of suffering. Due to this attachment, [worldly people continue to] live in the prison of the three realms[68] and do not seek for liberation; it is as if they are irrational." Consequently, the Buddha patiently and repeatedly expounded various explanations and parables on the Four Noble Truths. The primary purpose for doing so is to instruct ordinary people that, "Suffering should be known, the cause of suffering should be eliminated, the cessation of suffering should be actualized; [and] for these three goals, the path should be practiced" (*Treatise on the Four Noble Truths*).

Development of the Mahayana's Four Universal Vows

Apart from having the Four Noble Truths to explain the phenomena of the universe, the main objective of the Buddha's teachings is to solve the problems in life. Therefore, it is inadequate to speak on the Four Noble Truths without any implementation. The Four Noble Truths instruct that it requires action to sever the cause of suffering in order to eliminate suffering; it takes action to practice the path to arrive at the cessation of suffering. Consequently, the Four Universal Vows and the six perfections, which are derived from the Four Noble Truths, are the skillful means for us to arrive at liberation.

Essentially, the Four Universal Vows are the vows to attain liberation. Upholding these vows, the bodhisattva pledges to benefit all sentient beings, actualize the Truth, and reach enlightenment. Therefore, the process from the Four Noble Truths to the Four Universal Vows is one that occurs naturally, methodically, and purposefully. Consequently, with the Four Universal Vows complimenting the Four Noble Truths, our practice would be more complete and effective.

When we understand "suffering" and yet do not vow to eliminate it, how will we be able to practice and be a bodhisattva? Likewise, when we understand the "cause of suffering" and yet do not vow to eradicate it, how will we then enter into the Path? As such, if we are equipped with Dharma knowledge but do not apply it in practice, we are not only limited to the inability to attain Buddhahood but we will also be unable to solve simple problems in life.

In essence, if we are unable to enter the Path, we will be incapable of realizing the bodhisattva vows. Therefore, following an in-depth comprehension of Early Buddhism's[69] Four Noble Truths, we should proceed to make the Four Universal Vows and implement them. When we are confronted by innumerable sentient beings in suffering, particularly by the torments of birth and death, how could we not have the compassion to vow for the liberation of these beings? Similarly, when we are witness to the cause of suffering of sentient beings and how their minds are bound by affliction and karma, how could we not have the compassion to vow for the removal of those restrictions, and in turn, assist sentient beings to achieve a free and easy life? How could we not also help these sentient beings experience complete liberation from all forms of suffering?

Of course, it is not easy to eliminate the cause of suffering and be free from suffering. In order to do so, we not only rely on the power of our vows[70] but are also dependent on other's vows[71] to guide us in our practice; to be free from suffering, eliminate the cause of suffering, and attain nirvana. The power of vows is also emphasized in the *Treatise on Perfection of the Great Wisdom* (*Mahaprajnaparamita Sastra*),[72] which documents "If building merits without vows, one will be directionless and without standards. With vows serving as guidance, one could then have achievement. For example, the shape of a gold piece depends on the creativity of the goldsmith, for gold originally has no pre-determined shape." The treatise further states, "Adorning the Buddha Land requires great effort. Individual virtues and merits are incomplete; thus, one should rely on the power of vows to achieve successfully. For although the cow can pull the cart, a driver is required to guide the direction of the cart."

Consequently, we can attain enlightenment through either the "worldly path"[73] or the "transcendental path."[74] We can also do so through either the "path of five vehicles" or the "path of Mahayana."[75] In addition, there are also the thirty-seven practices to enlightenment (*bodhipaksika*),[76] which includes the four applications of mindfulness (*satipatthana*),[77] four right efforts (*samyak-prahana*),[78] four bases of spiritual power (*riddhipada*),[79] five faculties (*indriya*),[80] five powers (*bala*),[81] seven limbs of enlightenment (*sapta-bodhyangani*),[82] and the Eightfold Noble Path. Hence, how could we not fully utilize these supreme Dharma teachings that would ultimately lead us to Buddhahood?

In short, after understanding the Four Noble Truths, we need to learn the bodhisattva's way of not abandoning any sentient beings. We also need to apply the fundamentals of the Four Noble Truths and practice the Four Means of Embracing (*catvari-sam-graha-vastuni*)[83] and the six perfections. As a result, we would then be able to fulfill the Four Universal Vows of the bodhisattva path. As Master Xingan[84] states, "The key to enter the path is to have the right intention while the first stage in practice is to make vows. Through vows, sentient beings could be liberated, and through the right intention, Buddhahood could be realized"(*Inspiration for the Bodhicitta Pledge*). [85]

As demonstrated above, our entrance into the path is the result of the fulfillment of vows. Without the guide of a vow, how can we reach the pristine Buddha Land? Therefore, having the bodhicitta inspiration and making vows are essential conditions to all achievements. Not only has the power of vows been implied in Buddhist sutras, some clearly document that without the power of vows, no Buddhas could have attained their respective Buddhahood.

For instance, Amitabha Buddha[86] made forty-eight great vows to accomplish his Pure Land (*The Larger Sutra on Amitayus* [*Sukhavativyuha*],[87] fas. 1). Sakyamuni Buddha made five hundred great vows to attain Buddhahood (*Karunapundarika Sutra*,[88] fas. 7). Maitreya Bodhisattva[89] fulfilled ten great vows to be the next Buddha to come to this saha world (*Sutra of the Questions Asked by Maitreya*)[90]. To eliminate the suffering of sentient beings, Bhaisajyaguru Buddha (Medicine Buddha)[91] made twelve great vows and, consequently, accomplished the Pure Land of Azure Radiance[92] (*Sutra of Medicine Buddha*)[93]. Manjusri Bodhisattva's[94] twelve great vows enabled him to attain prajna. Samantabhadra Bodhisattva[95] made ten great vows to achieve the worlds of Flower Ornament (*Flower Ornament Sutra*). Avalokitesvara Bodhisattva[96] made ten great vows to liberate sentient beings from the ocean of suffering (*Lotus Sutra* [*Saddharmapundarika Sutra*])[97]. Lastly, Ksitigarbha Bodhisattva[98] vowed that "till hell is vacant, Buddhahood will not be achieved; till all sentient beings are liberated, bodhi will not be actualized." (*Sutra on the Past Vows of the Earth Store Bodhisattva* [*Ksitigarbhapranidhana Sutra*])[99].

This clearly demonstrates that the vows made by the Buddhas and bodhisattvas are consistently within the paradigm of the Four Universal Vows. This can be further illustrated through Samantabhadra Bodhisattva's ten great vows. His sixth vow, "Imploring the turning of the Dharma Wheel," and his ninth vow, "Always obliging to the needs of sentient beings," are parallel to the Universal Vow, "Sentient beings are infinite, I vow to liberate them." Samantabhadra's fourth vow, "Repenting all unwholesome karmas," is synonymous to the Universal Vow, "Afflictions are infinite, I vow to eradicate them." His fifth vow, "Rejoicing in others' merits and virtues," and eighth vow, "Always learning the dharmas," are equivalent to the Universal Vow, "Dharmas are in exhaustible, I vow to study them." Finally, Samantabhadra's first vow, "Paying homage to all Buddhas," his second vow, "Praising the Tathagatas,"[100] his third vow, "Extensive practicing of offerings," his seventh vow, "Imploring the presence of Buddhas in the world," and his tenth vow, "Transferring of merits and virtues to all sentient beings," are similar to the Universal Vow, "Buddhahood is supreme, I vow to obtain it."

Therefore, the Four Universal Vows are the definitive of all the bodhisattvas' vows. Throughout various Buddhist sutras and commentaries, the context and explication of the Four Universal Vows are recorded in different manners:

(1) *The Sixth Patriarch Platform Sutra*[101] –
i. "Sentient beings are infinite, I vow to liberate them."
ii. "Afflictions are infinite, I vow to eradicate them."
iii. "Dharmas are inexhaustible, I vow to study them."
iv. "Buddhahood is supreme, I vow to obtain it."
[This version of the Four Universal Vows is the most well known.]

(2) *Sutra on the Practice of Prajnaparamita* (fas. 8, ch. 28)[102] –
i. "Those who have not crossed to the other shore, I

shall deliver them."

ii. "Those who have not ended their suffering, I shall help them end it."

iii. "Those who have fear, I shall assuage them."

iv. "Those who have not attained nirvana, I shall help them attain it."

(3) *Lotus Sutra* (fas. 3, ch. 5) –

i. "Those who have not crossed over, I will enable them to cross."

ii. "Those who have not been freed, I will free them."

iii. "Those who are not at peace, I will put them at peace."

iv. "Those who are not in nirvana, I will enable them to enter nirvana."

(4) *Medallion Sutra on the Bodhisattva Path* (fas.1) –
In this sutra, the Four Universal Vows are stated in relation to the Four Noble Truths. Hence, according to this sutra, the Four Universal Vows are:

i. "To enable those who are not free from suffering, to be free."

ii. "To enable those who do not understand the cause

of suffering, to understand it."

iii. "To enable those who have not practiced the path, to practice it."

iv. "To enable those who have not attained nirvana, to attain it."

In other words, the Four Universal Vows are the force behind the Four Noble Truths toward Buddhahood.

(5) *The Collection of Dharanis*[103] (fas. 3) –

i. "The mind that is as vast as the earth," implies that the vows of the bodhisattvas are capable of cultivating the wholesome seeds of all sentient beings.

ii. "The mind that is as expedient as a bridge or ship," suggests that the vows of the bodhisattvas are capable of helping sentient beings to cross over to the other shore.

iii. "The mind that is as expansive as the ocean," signifies that the vows of the bodhisattvas are capable of nurturing all sentient beings, and together, they reach the source of Truth.

iv. "The body that is as limitless as the sky," infers that the vows of the bodhisattvas are capable of embracing all existence, and in unison with all sentient beings, they actualize Buddha Nature.

(6) *The Great Techniques of Stopping [Delusion] and Seeing [Truth]*[104] –

The Four Universal Vows as stated in this text are identical to the Platform Sutra except for one word. In the Platform Sutra, it is stated, "Dharmas are inexhaustible, I vow to study them." In contrast, The Great Techniques documents the same vow as, "Dharmas are inexhaustible, I vow to understand them." This dissimilarity is possibly due to the difference in word preference by either Patriarch [referring to the Patriarchs, Huineng and Zhiyi].

(7) *The Ceremonial Procedures for Transmission of the Bodhicitta Precepts*[105] –

In this Tantric sutra, the translator, who had a different perspective on the Four Universal Vows, expanded them to five vows as:
i. "Sentient beings are infinite, I vow to liberate them."
ii. "Merits and wisdom are infinite, I vow to obtain them."
iii. "Dharmas are infinite, I vow to study them."

iv. "Tathagatas are infinite, I vow to serve them."
v. "Buddhahood is supreme, I vow to obtain it."

(8) The Japanese Tendai School[106] –

The Four Universal Vows of the Japanese Tendai School are identical to those of the Chinese Tientai School. This demonstrates that Japanese Buddhism inherited its teachings from Chinese Buddhism, while adhering to the rules of translating sutras and preserving their original interpretation.

According to the *Surangama Sutra*,[107] "If the seed is impure, the fruit will be imperfect." Henceforth, it is essential when making vows that they be characterized by greatness, pureness, completeness, and trueness. In other words, it is vital that the vows are made without the distraction of worldly desires, fame, and power. Furthermore, even when confronted with life's difficult challenges, i.e., life and death, we must never disregard the vows that we have made. Only with a single-minded commitment to attaining Buddhahood and liberating sentient beings when making our vows will we not deviate from the path.

In the *Glossary of Translated Terms*,[108] elucidates that practicing Buddhism requires the inspiring of the three states of mind, i.e., "the mind of great wisdom," "the mind of great compassion," and "the mind of great vow." Similarly, *The Way to Buddhahood*[109] affirms that the basis of practicing the bodhisattva way is comprised of three principles, i.e., "the mind of wisdom," "the mind of kindness and compassion," and "the mind of bodhi." Thus, the "inspiring of the three states of mind" means to follow the Four Universal Vows and to rely primarily on the bodhi mind, not only to ultimately attain Buddhahood but also to liberate all sentient beings. This is due to:

(1) Sentient beings are infinite, I vow to liberate them –

As suggested by the Buddhist adage, "Teaching the Dharma as my duty, and benefiting sentient beings as my mission," we as Buddhists must not only seek personal liberation, but also need to assume the responsibility of teaching the Dharma and liberating sentient beings. Therefore, as long as we practice according to the Mahayana path, we must make the vow, "Sentient beings are infinite, I vow to liberate them."

However, while privately it is easy to inspire or make such a vow, to inspire or make such a vow when in the presence of the Buddhas and sentient beings would be more formidable. As such, to liberate sentient beings is not merely providing them with food when hungry or dispensing medication when they are sick. This is because the provision of food and care will not bring lasting meaningful benefits to sentient beings, as these superficial provisions will not enhance their wisdom nor help them escape from the cycle of birth and death.

The *Diamond Sutra* [*Vajracchedika Prajnaparamita Sutra*][110] states "Whether they be born from eggs, from wombs, from moisture, or from transmutation; whether they have form or have no form; whether they have perception, have no perception, or neither have nor do not have perception, I will lead them to nirvana. And when these innumerable, infinite sentient beings have been led to nirvana, in truth, I realize none have been liberated." Hence, the ability to liberate all sentient beings with the most supreme mind and boundless inspiration of the mind, yet without any attachment or discrimination, is then truly "Sentient beings are infinite, I vow to liberate them."

(2) Afflictions are infinite, I vow to eradicate them –

Practicing Buddhism is, in fact, fighting a battle with our afflictions. Once our afflictions have been conquered, our suchness[111] will naturally be revealed and we will be directed toward Buddhahood. On the contrary, if we cannot even end our own afflictions, not only are we unable to escape the suffering sea of birth and death, merely the thought of liberating sentient beings will be futile. Consequently, foremost in practicing Buddhism is to have a good well being and accomplish the cessation of all afflictions.

Afflictions exist because their commander-in-chief is our attachment to ego. Beneath the rank of the commander, there are generals known as greed, hatred, and ignorance leading the troops. The leader of the next rank below the generals is called "middle afflictions." Finally, the foot soldiers at the bottom of the rank are named "accessory afflictions."[112] Within this hierarchy, the total sum of afflictions numbers eighty-four thousand kinds. In view of this, we are indeed vulnerable. If we rely only on ourselves to contend with the eighty-four thousand afflictions without the support of great vows, a single carelessness will cause us to lose the whole battle and drown and perish in our sea of afflictions forever. Is this not regrettable?

(3) Dharmas are inexhaustible, I vow to study them –

Since having the mind of liberating all sentient beings is significant in practicing Buddhism, we must first equip ourselves with various kinds of knowledge and special skills. In ancient Indian Buddhism, there was the well known five courses of study (*vidyas*),[113] which includes *sabdavidya* (linguistic, phonology, literary studies, and music), *sil-*

pasthanavidya (science technology, arts, and crafts) *cikitsadvidya* (medicine and public health), *hetuvidya* (logic and reasoning), and *adhyatmavidya* (inner science, metaphysics, and psychology).

Although the five *vidyas* described above appear to provide extensive knowledge, they alone are insufficient for the diversity of people in contemporary society. However, this is only to emphasize that bodhisattvas must acquire such extensive knowledge to liberate all sentient beings. Furthermore, bodhisattvas in modern society need also arm themselves with the knowledge of science, psychology, management, and information technology.

The *Flower Ornament Sutra* actively encourages bodhisattvas to study and learn extensively. On the other hand, in our mundane world, the study of linguistics and archeology are already complicated subject areas. In addition to such magnitude of difficulty, the *Tripitaka* of sutra, vinaya, and abhidharma (or commentaries), the three studies of precepts, concentration, and wisdom in Buddhist doctrines, as well as various kinds of teachings and methods of all the Buddhist schools must also be learnt. Therefore, as modern Buddhist practitioners, we must not discriminate against others or other teachings. As long as the teachings are not heresies, but are in accordance with the "six sense organs"[114] and the "eight consciousness"[115] [*astau vijnanani*], why should we value only our own and belittle others?

(4) Buddhahood is supreme, I vow to attain it –

The ultimate goal in practicing Buddhism is to attain Buddhahood. However, achieving Buddhahood is not easy, because it takes three great *kalpas*[116] to cultivate merits and wisdom, and a hundred *kalpas*[117] to cultivate the "supreme marks."[118] Indeed, people today are easily discouraged as soon as they learn that the road to Buddhahood is a long and arduous one. Moreover, if we do not pursue this goal with a single-minded determination, perseverance, and courage, Buddahood will certainly be difficult to achieve. Henceforth, in the *Lotus Sutra*, it states that the Buddha[119] established "conjured city" in order to receive fearful and fragile sentient beings and subsequently enabled them to accomplish the path.

In reality, the premise for the Buddha's achievement of his Buddhahood was not only due to his birth in the human world, his renunciation, and his practice of ascetism, but also by his contention and finally the subduing of maras.[120] In this context, maras imply the external seductions of sounds, senses, forms, and material gains, as well as the internal forces of greed, hatred, and ignorance. In the midst of a life and death crisis, it is possible for us to be fearful and vulnerable. Consequently, when in such precarious state, we are easily overcome by maras. In short, although achieving Buddhahood is not easy, we still need to achieve it so that we are able to treasure the Buddhist path even more.

The Implementation from the Four Noble Truths to the Four Universal Vows

In Mahayana Buddhism, the Four Universal Vows are the deep commitment and great promises, which developed from the Four Noble Truths. Within the *Great Techniques of Stopping [Delusion] and Seeing [Truth]* (fas. 1), Master Zhiyi[121] describes that the Four Universal Vows are borne out from the profundity of the Four Noble Truths. Master Zhiyi further states that the Mahayana bodhisattvas whose bodhi mind has arisen as a result of learning and practicing the Four Noble Truths, need to fulfill the bodhisattva path and also expound the true essence of the Four Universal Vows based on the Four Noble Truths.

The *Bodhisattva Medallion Sutra*[122] affirms, "If there are any good men or good women who can accept, uphold, and recite the Four Noble Truths, they will serve as the field of merits for others. Why is this so? World Honored One,[123] the good men and good women made such great vows not for their own benefits, but because they are motivated to liberate all sentient beings in the universe, and they will not enter mahaparinirvana until all sentient beings have attained the realm of parinirvana." From this passage, it clearly shows that the Four Universal Vows already exist in the sphere of the Four Noble Truths.

Furthermore, in the *Agama Sutras*,[124] the Buddha frequently utilized terms such as "vast," "infinite," and "supreme" to convey the teachings, as he would when expounding the Four Universal Vows. For example, when the Buddha delivered a significant teaching, he exhorted, "I have discoursed the Dharma widely and demonstrated the benefit of this teaching...You should uphold it and speak of it widely to others" (*Long Discourses of the Buddha [Dirghagama]*,[125] fas. 3); or "With sincerity, I discoursed the Dharma and spread the Dharma vastly to let all directions be filled with the Dharma" (*Middle Length Discourses of the Buddha*, fas. 54); or "Those bhiksus and bhiksunis who practice the 'four bases of spiritual powers' (*riddhipada*), extensively expound and demonstrate its meaning" (*Gradual Discourses of the Buddha*, fas. 18); or "I and others[126] frequently instruct the Dharma, namely the Four Noble Truths; employing incalculable skillful techniques to contemplate and explore it, realize its respective meanings, and finally, expound it widely to people" (*Gradual Discourses of the Buddha*, fas.19).

Likewise, among the Buddha's disciples and throughout numerous situations, various terms corresponding to the above were used. For instance, upon hearing the teaching, the disciples exclaimed, "I learned this teaching and have a wide understanding of its meaning" (*Middle Length Discourses of the Buddha*, fas. 49, ch. 191). When referring to cultivation, "The wholesome dharmas, which have arisen, should forever be in our abode without being forgotten or regressed; with increasing, boundless practicing and learning, [they] should be completed" (*Middle Length Discourses of the Buddha*, fas. 60, ch. 222). Others include, "Such as the mind that is full of compassion, joy, and equanimity, free of hatred, resentment, anger, and contention, is one that is immensely vast and exceedingly great; that which is tantamount to countless wholesome cultivation; or that which is also comparable to the expanse of achievements throughout the universe" (*Middle Length Discourses of the Buddha*, fas. 60, ch. 218); or "[Observing the 'eight precepts'[127]] is exceedingly vast and great and not expectant of any reward. The wise praises [it] as having completeness, good tendencies, excellent perception, and wholesome fulfillment" (*Middle Length Discourses of the Buddha*, fas. 55, ch. 202); or "If there are believers in *brahmana*[128] and laity who go to the numerous gardens[129] to make widespread offerings and cultivate merits, I and others will extend our hands fully to receive" (*Middle Length Discourses of the Buddha*, fas. 50, ch. 192); or "If there are beneficiaries [of offerings] who received clothing, food, bedding, medicine, and various necessities of life, the almsgiver will gain immense blessings, good fruits, virtues and merits, as well as rewards" (*Middle Length Discourses of the Buddha*, fas. 48, ch. 182); or

"Bhiksus, remember to benefit self, others, and the multitudes. [Remember] to be empathetic to all existence in the world, by aiding the universe and human beings in seeking righteousness, benefits, inner peace, and happiness. Bhiksus, such an insightful bhiksu is one with wise intelligence and great wisdom" (*Middle Length Discourses of the Buddha*, fas. 45, ch. 172); or "Bhiksus, study extensively the abundant knowledge and teachings, uphold them, do not forget them, gather them, and profoundly comprehend them" (*Middle Length Discourses of the Buddha*, fas. 36, ch. 145); or "Contemplating on the Enlightened One and his tender golden body,[130] the wild could be tamed. It could also vastly liberate the wanderers"[131] (*Connected Disccourses of the Buddha*, fas. 44); or "The gathas spoken by the elders and the bhiksunis, the shilu gatha, the *Atthakavagga*,[132] the *muni* gatha, and the sutras, are all widely recited" (*Connected Discourses of the Buddha*, fas. 49); or "Because [I] know all sentient beings are inclined to attachment and unwholesome roots, [I] decide to liberate myself and extensively liberate all sentient beings" (*Connected Discourses of the Buddha*, fas. 48); or "Sentient beings are unaware of the Tathagata's words and teachings. [You] should frequently make offerings to the mass, especially to places of purified practitioners. [Your] mind and nature, which are pure, will gain multiple merits and blessings. Offering the merits equally, [you] will receive great rewards. The reward from what you offered is excellent! This mind is toward the great field of merits" (*Gradual Discourses of the Buddha*, fas.4); or "There are the 'Four Methods Related to Right Thought,' which comprised of 'the method of uncomplicated thinking,' 'the method of comprehensive thinking,' 'the method of limitless thinking,' and 'the method of thinking without conceptualization'" (*Long Discourses of the Buddha*, fas.8); or "The mind of loving-kindness is great, without duality, is limitless, without hatred, and extends throughout the world" (*Long Discourses of the Buddha*, fas.8).

The Buddha did not only exhort his disciples to carry out "boundless practicing and learning" and to make "widespread offerings and cultivate merits," but when elaborating aspects on virtues, merits, loving-kindness, and vows, he also mentioned, "immeasurable virtues and merits," "incalculable blessings," "boundless wholesomeness," "practicing the four immeasurable states of mind," "infinite joy," "loving-kindness is great, without duality, and is limitless," "the method of limitless thinking," "infinite afflictions," "liberating the infinite sentient beings," "the immeasurable and the boundless," "learn vastly," "inexhaustible wisdom," "immense inner peace and happiness," "immeasurable state of mind," "to give sentient beings immense joy," "inexhaustible consolation," "infinite longevity," "immense happiness," "infinite life," and "incalculable wholesome cultivation."

Furthermore, to describe the superiority of the Dharma, the Buddha used expressions such as, "the supreme Dharma Wheel," "the excellent enlightenment," "the Buddha is the most Honored One," "the Tathagata of foremost wisdom," "seeking the accomplishment of the supreme path," "the ultimate attainment," "the greatest practice of purity," "the supreme precepts," "the most highly respected," "the most remembered," "the Supreme One," "attaining the supreme path," "the perfect bodhi," and "the utmost purity."

In conclusion, the above phrases clearly demonstrate that the philosophy of the Mahayana School is profoundly implicated within the Agama Sutras. In other words, the Four Universal Vows, which are a major component of the Mahayana teaching, can also be found within the *Agama Sutras*.

A verse from the *Gradual Discourses of the Buddha Sutra* reads, "The Tathagata has terminated his 'outflows' (*asrava*),[133] achieved the state of 'without outflows' (*anasrava*),[134] attained the liberation of mind[135] and the liberation of wisdom,[136] [become] free from the cycle of birth and death, completed pure cultivation, accomplished all that needs to be done, and is not subjected to anymore rebirth" (fas. 42, ch. 46). Similarly, in the *Connected Discourses of the Buddha*, it records, "All outflows have been terminated, accomplished all that needs to be done, relinquished the karma, [become] free from entanglements [of afflictions]; and the wonderful liberation is accomplished through the mind of prajna-wisdom" (fas. 50).

The illustrations above bear evidence to the existence of the Four Universal Vows within the *Agama Sutras*, i.e., "free from the cycle of birth and death" relates to "sentient beings are infinite, I vow to liberate them;" "relinquished the heavy burden" corresponds with "afflictions are inexhaustible, I vow to eradicate them;" "completed pure cultivation" parallels "Dharmas are inexhaustible, I vow to study them;" and "accomplished all that needs to be done" is equivalent to "Buddhahood is supreme, I vow to obtain it."

However, apart from the illustrations above, the basis of the Four Universal Vows is also represented in the *Agama Sutras*, including the following:

(1) Sentient beings are infinite, I vow to liberate them –

"[Utilizing] incalculable expedient means to teach [you] the Dharma, to exhort and inspire the admiration [for the Dharma], and to accomplish the [Dharma] joy [for you]. ...with regret, repentance, and the mind of compassion, [you should] benefit all, not excluding even insects; as a result, jealousy and hatred will be extinguished from [your] minds" (*Middle Length Discourses of the Buddha*, fas. 3, ch. 16).

"[To be] not confused with the truth of suffering, the truth of the cause of suffering, the truth of the cessation of suffering, and the truth of the path leading to the cessation of suffering. ...abandoning the knives and clubs; with regret, repentance, and the mind of compassion, [you should] benefit all not excluding even insects. ...to eliminate that which is not in accord with pure cultivation from [your] minds" (*Middle Length Discourses of the Buddha*, fas. 11, ch. 62).

"Now, I have benefited self, others, and the mass; empathized with all existence in the world, and assisted the universe and human beings in seeking righteousness, benefits, inner peace, and happiness" (*Middle Length Discourses of the Buddha*, fas. 11, ch. 62).

"Those who have faith enable [others] to believe in their faith and to establish their faith; [so do] those who practice the pristine precepts. Those who are stingy [should be taught] with giving, and those who have unwholesome intelligence [should be taught] with wholesome wisdom, to establish [theirs respectively]" (*Connected Discourses of the Buddha*).

"The Tathagata inexhaustibly comforts all sentient beings with compassion and empathy, as well as praises those who comfort all sentient beings with compassion and empathy. ...the Dharma spoken by the World Honored One I completely accept and uphold, allowing me to inexhaustibly utilize the teachings to give benefits, inner peace, and happiness [to sentient beings]" (*Connected Discourses of the Buddha*, fas. 32).

"If an upasaka[137] has achieved the 'sixteen states of practice,'[138] he is then known as the 'upasaka who pacified [the mind of] self and others'. ...If an upasaka is completely equipped with the correct faith, he can help others establish such faith. If an upasaka upholds the pristine precepts, he can help others establish such precepts" (*Connected Discourses of the Buddha*, fas. 33).

"Thus, the true teachings are revealed, which end the stream of birth and death. ...[first] contemplate on benefiting self, others, and both self and others; [then] practice diligently" (*Connected Discourses of the Buddha*, fas. 44).

"Bhiksus who have achieved the 'eleven states of practice'[139] are able to attain peace and joy, as well as helping others to similar attainments" (*Connected Discourses of the Buddha*, fas. 47).

"The Tathagata manifests in this world for five purposes. What are these five purposes? Firstly, to turn the Dharma Wheel. Secondly, to liberate his parents. Thirdly, to establish faith in those without faith. Fourthly, to inspire the bodhisattva mind in those who have not given rise to the bodhisattva mind. [And] fifthly, to foretell the future Buddhas-to-come. Therefore, when the Tathagata manifests in this world, it is for these five purposes" (*Gradual Discourses of the Buddha*, fas. 27).

"All World Honored Ones unceasingly practice compassion on those with forms. Now that they have done so, you, who are sitting peacefully and joyously under the trees, should practice diligently without indolence" (*Gradual Discourses of the Buddha*, fas. 30).

"All World Honored Ones have actualized great compassion. With the strength of great compassion, they instruct the Dharma to benefit sentient beings" (Gradual Discourses of the Buddha, fas. 31). "[If] there is one person who is not liberated, I will not abandon [him/her] regardless" (*Gradual Discourses of the Buddha*, fas. 33).

"With the guidance of good Dharma friends, I have also accomplished the supreme enlightenment and become the Enlightened One. Having arrived at the fruit of the path, I have liberated innumerable sentient beings, allowing them to be eternally free from birth, aging, illness, and death" (*Gradual Discourses of the Buddha*, fas. 40).

"[Practicing] the Four Immeasurable States of Mind,[140] [my] entire, incalculable, and limitless conduct will be protected. [Thus] the conducts of [my] body, speech, and mind will also be purified" (*Gradual Discourses of the Buddha*, fas. 40).

"At this time, the Tathagata's titles are widely known as Thus Come One (*Tathagata*), Worthy of Offerings (*Arhat*), Fully Enlightened One (*Samyuksambuddha*), Perfect Clarity and Conduct (*Vidyacarana-sampanna*), Well Gone (*Sugata*), Knower of the World (*Lokavid*), Supreme One (*Anuttara*), Teacher of People (*Purusa-damya-sarathi*), Teacher of Heavenly and Human Beings (*Sasta devamanusyanam*), Awakened One (*Buddha*), [and] Blessed One (*Bhagavan*).[141] He manifests in the world and liberates immeasurable sentient beings" (*Gradual Discourses of the Buddha*, fas. 46).

"Now, what the honored one[142] had [just]

spoken on, using limitless expedient means [is difficult to understand and fulfill]. [But] now, we take refuge in the Buddha, the Dharma, and the Sangha, and upon listening to the honored one, we [upasakas] can [only] pledge that [we] will eternally not take any life" (*Gradual Discourses of the Buddha*, fas. 46).

"[You], Sakyamuni Buddha, Thus Come One, Worthy of Offering, Fully Enlightened One, bear compassion for all sentient beings, [just] as a mother who cares for her children without discrimination. ...The teachings spoken by the Tathagata are absolute and without a doubt; [they] also bear compassion for all sentient beings and have liberated sentient beings" (*Gradual Discourses of the Buddha*, fas. 47).

"The Tathagata has given infinite benefits to sentient beings, bestowed inner peace and joy to sentient beings, and with compassion brought boundless benefits to heavenly and human beings. Neither in the past, present, nor future, is there one apart from the Buddha who is able to benefit and give inner peace and joy to sentient beings" (*Long Discourses of the Buddha*, fas. 5).

(2) Afflictions are infinite, I vow to eradicate them –

"The widely learned noble disciples who have departed from the wrong views and have eliminated them; who are engaged in right view without inversion. ...[Having accomplished] self-awareness and self-enlightenment, they [are capable of] validating their respective achievement. [And] they have also removed [all] wrong views from their minds" (*Middle Length Discourses of the Buddha*, fas. 3, ch. 16).

"If the Honored Teacher joyfully resides in [the state of] renunciation, and the secondary and tertiary disciples[143] also emulated [his] renunciation, then, such [behavior of] the secondary and tertiary disciples could be praised. If the Honored Teacher exhorts on the way to eliminate the wrong views, and the secondary and tertiary disciples [also adhered to] the ways to end them, then, such [behavior of] the secondary and tertiary disciples could be praised" (*Middle Length Discourses of the Buddha*, fas. 22, ch. 88).

"Enable those sentient beings with impurities to be purified; enable those sentient beings with purity to be purified again" (*Connected Discourses of the Buddha*, fas. 30).

"Since beginningless time [sentient beings] are in never-ending birth and death, and continuously in transmigration; [yet, they] do not know the cause for the suffering [of birth and death]. Therefore, bhiksus! [You] should learn to eliminate the karma [of birth and death] and do not allow it to increase" (*Connected Discourses of the Buddha*, fas. 38).

"If greed has been completely eradicated, if hatred has been completely eradicated, if ignorance has been completely eradicated, and all afflictions have been completely eradicated, it is called arhatship" (*Connected Discourses of the Buddha*, fas. 41).

"These five aggregates have been completely eliminated and will never emerge [anymore]; this state is called extinction (*vyupasana*)" (*Gradual Discourses of the Buddha*, fas. 26).

"[You should also] terminate the outflows, achieve [the state of] without outflows, and attain the liberation of mind as well as the liberation of wisdom. In this world, [you should] make an exemplar of yourself and instruct [sentient beings everywhere] to deliver them from a state of delusion to the state of awakening" (*Gradual Discourses of the Buddha*, fas. 39).

"Any unwholesome thought should be relinquished. Thus, bhiksu! [You] should practice such" (*Gradual Discourses of the Buddha*, fas. 40).

"There are the 'ten contemplations,'[144] which are extensive [but] should be practiced individually, in order to terminate all passions of desire, form, formlessness, arrogance, and ignorance" (*Gradual Discourses of the Buddha*, fas. 42).

"In this world, the extinction of outflows has been attained. [This is] also the extinction of any future outflows [which] cause [all] diseases" (*Gradual Discourses of the Buddha*, fas. 42).

"[You] should remember to abandon the 'ten unwholesome conducts'[145] and practice the 'ten wholesome conducts.'[146] Thus, bhiksus! [You] should practice such" (*Gradual Discourses of the Buddha*, fas. 43).

"What are the 'seven techniques to understand the Dharma'?[147] They are [also] called the 'seven diligences,' i.e., diligence in upholding precepts, diligence in eliminating greed, diligence in extinguishing wrong views..." (*Long Discourses of the Buddha*, fas. 9).

"Immaculately uphold the pure cultivation. In this world, [you should] make an exemplar of yourself - end birth and death, accomplish all that needs to be done, become no longer subject to anymore existences, [and] achieve arhatship" (*Long Discourses of the Buddha*, fas. 17).

(3) Dharma are inexhaustible, I vow to study them –
"This mind is full of loving-kindness, free of hatred, resentment, anger, and contention; [this mind]

is immensely vast and exceedingly great; that which is tantamount to countless wholesome cultivation; or that which is also comparable to the expanse of achievements throughout the universe" (*Middle Length Discourses of the Buddha*, fas. 3, ch. 15).

"The elder bhiksus have studied extensively the abundant knowledge. ...Thus, [you should also] study and learn widely such dharmas; joyfully comprehend [and practice] them thousands of times; think and contemplate their meanings; and [through them] reach profoundly to the intelligent views" (*Middle Length Discourses of the Buddha*, fas. 5, ch. 26).

"Bhiksus of 'unconditioned dharma'[148] practice unconditioned dharmas. ...[You] should learn to protect all your sense organs. ...[You] should learn to practice diligently without indolence. ...[You] should learn to have right thought and right wisdom. ...[You] should learn to manage time effectively. ...[You] should learn sitting [meditation] and its proper etiquette..." (*Middle Length Discourses of the Buddha*, fas.6, ch. 26).

"Because you have remorse and repentance, [you] attained the states of wholesomeness and abandonment. It is a wondrous [state of] extinction and quietude. Removing all karmas of existence, [being] free from attachment and without desires, completing annihilation [of unwholesomeness], and [attaining] the state without remainders (*niravasesa*).[149] Saints! [These] are known as the great lessons for bhiksus" (*Middle Length Discourses of the Buddha*, fas. 7, ch. 30).

"[You] should practice one teaching and instruct it extensively. [You, who] practice one teaching, has a good reputation, attains the wondrous fruit, is surrounded by wholesomeness, gains the sweet taste of dew, arrives at the state of awakening, acquires supernatural power, removes all delusional thoughts, obtains the fruit of sramana,[150] and arrives at nirvana. What is this teaching? It is the contemplation on the Buddha. ...[This teaching] that the Tathagata discourses on is the fundamental of all dharmas. We implore the World Honored One to speak this wondrous teaching to [us] bhiksus. Once we bhiksus have heard it from the Tathagata, we will uphold it" (*Gradual Discourses of the Buddha*, fas. 2).

"[You] should remember to constantly practice this teaching. In daily life, [you should] practice meditation and contemplation [on this teaching] without indolence" (*Gradual Discourses of the Buddha*, fas. 30).

"Bhiksus! You should always learn to have the right intention and remove [all] jealousy. You should cultivate [your] conduct and teach [only] that which is in accord with the Dharma" (*Gradual Discourses of the Buddha*, fas. 26).

"Bhiksus, you should know! My teaching is vastly profound, boundless, and bottomless; [it can] terminate [your] suspiciousness, [and it is] a wholesome dharma that brings inner peace. If there are good men and good women [with] wholeheartedness who completely [understand] this Dharma, even when their bodies are decaying, [their minds] remain engaged in the Dharma without forgetting. ...[You] should learn such!" (*Discourses of the Buddha*, fas. 42).

"You should diligently cultivate wholesome conducts. [If you] cultivate wholesome conducts, your longevity will increase; [your] complexion will improve; you will gain inner peace and happiness; [you] will receive abundant wealth; and obtain complete strength. ...Bhiksus, [you] should cultivate such wholesome [conducts]" (*Long Discourses of the Buddha*, fas. 6, ch. 6).

"First, contemplate on the body's internals with diligence, without indolence, with concentration, and without forgetting, which will remove worldly greed and worries; contemplate on the body's externals with diligence, without indolence, with concentration, and without forgetting; contemplate on both the body's internals and externals with diligence, without indolence, with concentration, and without forgetting" (*Long Discourses of the Buddha*, fas. 5, ch. 4).

"The bhiksu who has ended his outflows contemplates from every perspective. [He] truly comprehends, understands, and realizes. [As such] worldly greed, jealousy, evilness, and unwholesomeness will cease to arise. [In] practicing the four applications of mindfulness, [the bhiksu] practices and cultivates unreservedly. [In] practicing the five faculties, five powers, seven limbs of enlightenment, and the Eightfold Noble Path, [the bhiksu also] practices and cultivates unreservedly" (*Long Discourses of the Buddha*, fas. 9, ch. 10).

(4) Buddhahood is supreme, I vow to attain it –

"If there is an individual who does not like to contend, [he/she] is praised as honorable and a mediator of contention. Such practice is joyful, graceful, and likeable; [it] enables people to rejoice in it, respect it, learn and practice it, uphold it, achieve the state of sramana, accomplish [deep] concentration, and attain nirvana" (*Middle Length Discourses of the Buddha*, fas. 23, ch. 94).

"Departing from all defilements, attaining the path of nirvana, and finally, extinguishing all suffering, is called 'complete with virtues'" (*Connected Discourses of the Buddha*, fas. 35).

"[You] should be diligent and respectful. Focus your mind, have cautiousness, and relying on the strength of virtues, practice pure cultivation. [Regardless,] the elementary, intermediate, and advanced stages [should] have [achieved] the perfection of character. ...Until the state of nirvana without remainders, [you] should learn such" (*Connected Discourses of the Buddha*, fas. 47).

"Nirvana is the wholesome inclination of [the] bhiksus. Bhiksus! [You] should now pursue [the] expedient means to attain nirvana" (*Gradual Discourses of the Buddha*, fas. 26).

"To seek for the achievement of the path's-fruition, the abyss of birth and death is not the dwelling. To will for the attainment of nirvana, slothfulness is not the qualification" (*Gradual Discourses of the Buddha*, fas. 27).

"[You] should make vows; [for] without the vow, there will be no fruition. For this reason... if elder bhiksus do not make vows, [they] will not attain

Buddhahood" (*Gradual Discourses of the Buddha*, fas. 38).

"[You] should focus the mind without idleness. Also seek the expedient means to accomplish the Eightfold Noble Path. Following the Eightfold Noble Path, [you] can liberate yourself from the sea of birth and death" (*Gradual Discourses of the Buddha*, fas. 39).

"Donning the armor of compassion and loving-kindness, [I] conquered mara and its subordinates; sitting under the king of all trees, [I] achieved the supreme path. ...[You] should know that compassion is the foremost and [also] the most supreme Dharma! Ananda,[151] [you] should know why [it is] the most supreme Dharma. [Because] the one who practices compassion has immeasurable virtues, [you] should seek the expedient means to practice the mind of compassion" (*Gradual Discourses of the Buddha*, fas. 41).

"[Any] sentient beings who follow and practice the 'ten wholesome conducts' will be reborn in the heavenly realm.[152] [Any sentient beings] who practice the 'ten unwholesome conducts' will be reborn in the lower realms.[153] [Any sentient beings] who practice the 'ten contemplations' will attain the state of nirvana. ...Among these, [the method of] the 'tencontemplations,' which leads to nirvana, [should be] followed and practiced well" (*Gradual Discourses of the Buddha*, fas. 43).

Verses from the sutras quoted so far suggest that most of the people in the mundane world learn the path [leading to nirvana] through [their own] "causes and conditions,"[154] with suffering as the "dominant condition"[155] for learning the path. For example, when children are playing happily, they will not think of their parents; but, as soon as they are bullied or frustrated, they will cry for either parent. The same is true for students, subordinates, and disciples. When all are well and happy, none will go to their supervisors or teachers. Yet, in the face of difficulties that they are unable to resolve, they will immediately look for someone to lament to. While there must be a reason for their difficulties, those students or disciples would not investigate for those reasons, and instead, remain dwelling within the aftermath of their difficulties. Consequently, someone is required to direct them to the cause of their difficulties and inform them that the reason for their suffering is due to the culmination of karma. In short, because they experienced suffering and needed someone to help liberate them, this is the so-called "entering the path due to suffering."

Furthermore, when suffering, children need to have parents who are willing to resolve their difficulties. Likewise, in confusion, students need to have teachers who are willing to remove their confusions. Therefore, children and students who are suffering and seek the assistance of adults will need adults who are capable of providing such assistance to solve their predicaments and eliminate their suffering. As such, the Four Noble Truths, which begin with suffering and the cause of suffering, indeed need the power of the great vows to neutralize sufferings. This is the basis for the deep and profound relationship between the Four Noble Truths and the Four Universal Vows.

Sentient beings in suffering due to transmigration will, of course, seek the other safer and more secure shore. However, not knowing where to find the boat to ferry across is most painful. Therefore, with sages and saints, who are teachers [of sentient beings], acting as skippers of the boat of great vow that is fully equipped with life-saving equipment, they ferry the drowning sentient beings to the other shore. It is also the same for sentient beings who are lost and who are unable to find daylight as well as the way out. If there is a teacher who can lead them to learn the path, overcome hindrances, and see the brightness of nirvana, this is the cessation of suffering and the path leading to the cessation of suffering. To make this possible, we have to rely on the cause and condition provided by sages and saints who made the Four Universal Vows.

In Chinese Buddhism, the four great bodhisattvas are the embodiment of the Four Universal Vows. Not only are they able to eliminate suffering and the cause of suffering, they have also achieved the cessation of suffering and the path leading to the cessation of suffering. For instance:

(1) Due to the great compassion, Avalokitesvara Bodhisattva manifests in the worlds. He observes that worldly sentient beings suffer from the "three poisons" (greed, hatred, ignorance), and are innocent victims of the "seven disasters" (fire, flood, hurricanes, warfare, demons, imprisonment, and criminals). Therefore, the compassionate Avalokitesvara Bodhisattva answers the calls of suffering, rescues sentient beings from suffering, and fulfills their vows. In other words, this is also an actualization of the great vow, "Sentient beings are infinite, I vow to liberate them."

(2) With the strength of his great vow, Ksitigarbha Bodhisattva remains in the hell realm to liberate sentient beings. The suffering that exists in the hell realm is caused by greed, hatred, ignorance, arrogance, mountains filled with knife blades, and trees with sword-like leaves. It can also be said that suffering is the result of afflictions and the culmination

of karma. Hence, due to the effort of Ksitigarbha Bodhisattva and his great vow, the hell realm sees the light of the Buddha's teachings.

(3) Due to his great wisdom, Manjusri Bodhisattva is endowed with wondrous merits and virtues. Through his great wisdom and wondrous merits and virtues, sentient beings are able to return from evilness to righteousness, from delusion to awakening, from pain to joy, and from wrong to correct. He is also able to provide sentient beings with the necessary expedient means and teachings. Therefore, he represents "Dharmas are inexhaustible, I vow to study them."

(4) Due to the strength of his great practice, Samantabhadra Bodhisattva encourages [the practice] of respect for others, the virtue of praising others, the ability for joyful generosity to sentient beings, and for all to have remorse, repentance, and humility. Therefore, Samantabhadra Bodhisattva can lead [sentient beings] of the ten-thousand practices and return to the Pure Land. In other words, he liberates all sentient beings who are in suffering, and thus, this is "Buddhahood is supreme, I vow to obtain it."

From ancient times to the present, there have also been many great masters who made vows to "preserve the Dharma in the world and enable sentient beings to be free from suffering." For instance, Bhiksu Purna[156] risked his life to teach the Dharma in the frontier of India; Syamaka Bodhisattva[157] vowed to transform his tears into a great ocean to nourish sentient beings; Chan Master Guishan Lingyou[158] vowed to be an ox so that sentient beings would have something to depend on; and Chan Master Zhishun[159] cut his own flesh to save the life of a pheasant. These various great vows, some of which may involve the sacrificing of body and life, are made to realize the bodhisattva path. When the Buddha was practicing the bodhisattva path, there was an incident where he cut his flesh to feed a hawk, as well as the time when he offered himself as food for the mother tigress to feed her cubs. If not for the great vows, how could he make such sacrifices?

Other examples include Prince Sudana[160] who always obliged others' requests and would never go against others' wishes (giving); the young novice monk who would rather die than violate the precepts (upholding the precepts); Chan Master Baiyin[161] who would rather be punished than defend himself against false accusations (endurance); Chan Master Baizhang's[162] "a day without work is a day without food" (diligence); the many Chan Masters who would practice concentration and teach the Dharma rather than attempt to indulge in evilness (samadhi); as well as Master Xuanzang[163] and Master Taixu[164] who liberated sentient beings through their wise teaching (prajna). They should be our role models.

These illustrations are also exactly in accord with the BLIA's (Buddha's Light International Association) observance of the Fo Guang Samadhi, which reads, "I vow not for my own sake, nor for the sake of heavenly and worldly rewards, nor to achieve the paths of the sravaka and the pratyeka buddhas; nor to achieve the path of bodhisattva. I vow only to rely on the supreme path, to inspire the bodhicitta pledge, and together with all sentient beings, attain *anuttara-samyak-sambodhi*." Therefore, this verse demonstrates that through complete understanding of the Four Noble Truths, we are able to practice the Four Universal Vows effectively.

In conclusion, the completion of compassion, wisdom, vows, and practice is called "the Buddha." The combined achievement of the four great bodhisattvas' merits and virtues is to actualize the ideal world of perfect enlightenment and contemplation.

Conclusion

In essence, the Buddha delivered his teachings through two distinctive methods, "Teach relative to one's potential and prescribe according to one's illness." It can also be concluded that He employed either "the Dharma appropriate for the intended sentient beings" or "the Dharma critical to the sentient being's potentiality." More importantly, among the Buddha's approaches, the Four Reliances were established as our basis for learning the Dharma, i.e., rely on the Dharma and not the instructor; rely on its meaning and not the words; rely on the wisdom and not the knowledge; and rely on unconditioned dharmas and not on conditioned dharmas.

While there are several manners [of learning the Dharma], from the Four Noble Truths, the Three Dharma Seals, and the Twelve Links of Dependent Origination, to the Four Universal Vows, each method could only proceed according to its individual progress and agenda. Only when the rationale behind the progress and agenda has been understood, can the adaptable and comprehensible Dharma exist. Consequently, even though the Buddha would often speak on the same Dharma, he would apply different approaches of teaching as appropriate to the situation, location, and his audiences' potentiality. This is a demonstration of the Buddha's expertise in "teaching relative to one's potential and prescribing according to one's illness." This also explains why the Buddha would at times teach "existence" and at another "emptiness"; at times, "nature" and at another, "appearance"; at times, "inherent condition" and at another, "functionality." Therefore, in practicing Buddhism, we should not fixate on mere words. Instead, we should "rely on self, rely on the Dharma, and not rely on others."

In reality, Buddhahood is not impossible to achieve! If, from understanding the Four Noble Truths to the fulfillment of the Four Universal Vows, we are able to inspire and make vows in accordance with the Dharma, practice diligently without indolence, and accumulate blessings, virtues, and good conditions, then Buddhahood is within our reach.

Within the present Buddhist communities, various interpretations of the Dharma are asserted as a result of variable intelligence, ability, and understanding. Hence, our comprehension of the Dharma can be distinguished as either superficial or profound, precious or vague. This reasoning can be illustrated by the following story:

Once, there were two monks who lived respectively on the east and west side of a town. Both novice monks often had to go into town to run errands and buy groceries under the direction of their master. However, the novice monk from the west side was more clever than the novice monk from the east side.

One day, during one of their trips into town, the two novice monks came across each other at a crossroad. Upon seeing each other, the east side novice monk asked, "Where are you going today?"

The west side novice monk replied,

"Wherever my legs take me."

The east side novice monk was at a loss for words to the other monk's response. He later returned to the monastery and retold the incident to his master. The master scolded his disciple for the latter's stupidity, and reprimanded him for not asking the west side novice monk, "If your legs don't move, please may I ask, where are you going to go?"

Not long after this encounter, both novice monks came across each other again at the crossroad in town. Once again, the east side novice monk asked, "Where are you going today?"

To this, the west side novice monk answered, "Wherever the wind takes me."

Because the response was different than the previous one, the east-side novice monk was again speechless to reply to the other novice's statement. Upon returning to the monastery, the master of the east side novice monk once again blamed his disciple's stupidity for not asking, "If there is no wind, where are you going to go?"

There was nothing the novice monk from the east could do but wait for the next opportunity. Finally, one day, the two novice monks ran into each other again at the crossroad. This time, the east side novice monk asked confidently, "Where are you going today?"

Without any hesitation, the west side novice monk replied, "I am going to the market to buy groceries."

Although "going to the market to buy groceries" is a simple and common phrase, it took the novice monk from the east side several attempts to understand it. In a similar manner, it is not easy to understand the integration of the Mahayana and Theravada Schools through the Four Noble Truths and the Four Universal Vows. However, with comprehensive wisdom and realization, integration is certainly possible.

Endnotes

[1] **different levels of doctrines:** Because all sentient beings have different levels of understanding and perception, Sakyamuni Buddha, for cultivating all sentient beings and leading them to liberation, applied different strategies and explained the Truth from different aspects. The result was that later Buddhists divided those teachings into different categories such as the teachings of emptiness, the Middle Way, and Mind-Only. All of these doctrines were developed from the Truth that the Buddha awakened.

[2] **sentient beings:** Sanskrit (*Skt.*) "*sattvas.*" The beings with consciousness, including the celestial beings, asuras, humans, animals, hungry ghosts, and hellish beings. From the Mahayana view, all sentient beings inherently have Buddha Nature, and therefore possess the capacity to attain enlightenment, or Buddhahood.

[3] **karma:** Literally, work, action, or deed. All intentional actions produce fruits (effects). Good conduct results in good karmic effects; bad conduct results in bad karmic effects. Karma can be divided into three kinds: the karma of body, speech, and mind.

[4] **Dharmas:** Here it indicates the teachings of the Buddha. The word "dharma" has several meanings, which are determined by the contents. With a capital "D," it refers to the above meaning and the Ultimate Truth. As Dharma is applied or practiced in life, it means righteousness or virtues. With a lowercase "d," it means anything that can be thought of, experienced, or named; similar to phenomena.

[5] **The First Setting in Motion of the Wheel of the Dharma:** *Skt. "dharma-cakra-pravartana."* The forty-five years when the Buddha discoursed the Dharma are divided into three periods. The first period is when the Buddha instructs the teachings of the Four Noble Truths and the Eightfold Noble Path to the five bhiksus at Deer Park. The second period is when the Buddha discourses the teachings of wisdom (*prajna*), sutras, and emptiness. The third period is when the Buddha instructs the teachings of the Middle Way (*Madhyama-pratipad*), including the *Flower Ornament Sutra, Lotus Sutra, Nirvana Sutra* and *Srimala Sutra*.

[6] **Three Turnings of the Dharma Wheel:** It indicates the first time the Buddha sets in motion the Wheel of the Dharma. There are several different interpretations about when this first happened: 1) 14 days after the Buddha's enlightenment (*Ten Stages Sutra*, fas. 1). 2) 21 days (*Lotus Sutra*, fas. 1 and *Sutra of Cause and Effect*, fas. 3). 3) 42 days (*Four Part Vinaya*, fas. 31). 4) 56 days (*Five Part Vinaya*, fas. 15). 5) 57 days (*Treatise*

on the Perfection of Great Wisdom, fas. 7 & fas. 34.) Several sutras describe this Dharma assembly: 1) The Fascicle 15, the *Connected Discourses of the Buddha* (T: vol. 2, no. 99). 2) The *Sutra on the Three Turnings of the Dharma Wheel*, Ch. *Fo Shuo San Zhuan Falun Jing*, translated by Yijing (T: vol. 2, no. 110). 3) The *Sutra of Turning the Dharma Wheel*, Ch. *Fo Shuo Zhuan Falun Jing*, translated by An Shigao. The Pali Canon also has a section that discusses the Three Turnings of the Dharma Wheel (Section 2): Setting in Motion the Wheel of the Dharma in Chapter 56: *Saccasamyutta* (*Connected Discourses on the Truths*) of *Samyutta Nikaya*.

[7] **way of vowing:** In Buddhism, there are three kinds of nutriment on the path to liberation. All of them are important to those who are seeking liberation. The first nutriment is belief (*Skt. sraddha, prasada, adhimukti* or *bhakti*), believing in what the Buddha taught; the second is vow (*Skt. pranidhana*), making vows to practice the Buddha's teachings and achieve Buddhahood; and the third is practice (*Skt. carya* or *carita*), fulfilling what we vowed. According to the sutras, "vow" needs belief to guide one in the right direction of what should be vowed. The strength of the vow needs to be fulfilled through practice. Conversely, practice needs the vow to guide one's efforts.

[8] **way of practicing:** The third of the three nutriments. In Pure Land School, one needs to fulfill the vow one made through

practice. Then the one can be reborn to the Pure Land.

[9] **six perfections:** Also known as "six *paramitas*." In Sanskrit, "*paramita*" means "gone to the opposite shore," "transcendent," "complete attainment," and "transcendental virtue," according to the *Sanskrit-English Dictionary*. The six perfections include the perfections of giving (*dana*), upholding precepts (*sila*), patience (*ksanti*), diligence (*virya*), meditation (*dhyana*), and wisdom (*prajna*).

[10] **a multi-faceted religion:** Referring to how later Buddhism developed into the different schools, such as the eighteen schools in India, and the eight schools in China. Different schools arose in order to place emphasis on different viewpoints and aspects, as well as to meet the diverse needs of sentient beings.

[11] **Dependent Origination:** *Skt.* "*pratitya-samutpada*"; in Pali, "*paticca-samuppada*." It means that all conditioned dharmas (phenomena) do not come into existence independently, but only as a result of causes and conditions, thus, no phenomena possesses an independent self-nature; this concept also refers to "interdependence." There are twelve factors, called the Twelve Links of Dependent Origination; ignorance, mental-formation, consciousness, mind and form, the six sense bases, contact, feeling, craving, grasping, becoming, birth, and aging and death. This concept is the core principle of Buddhism.

[12] **the cycle of birth and death:** *Skt. "samsara"* or *"jatimarana."* Also known as transmigration. When sentient beings die, they are reborn in one of the six realms of existence (the realms of heaven, human, asura, animals, hungry ghost, and hell). The cycle is continuous and endless due to the karmic result of one's deeds.

[13] **parinirvana:** A synonym for "nirvana." It indicates the state of having completed all merits and perfections and eliminated all unwholesomeness. Usually, it is used to refer to the time when the Buddha physically passed away.

[14] **Aniruddha:** One of ten disciples of the Buddha. He is known as the foremost in divine-eye.

[15] ***Sutra of the Teachings Bequeathed by the Buddha:*** *Ch.: Fo Yijiao Jing* (T: vol. 12, no. 389). Translated into Chinese by Kumarajiva. It describes the Buddha's last teachings before he entered parinirvana. The teachings instruct the disciples to follow the pratimoksa, see it as the teacher, rely on it for guiding the five sense organs, and attaining freedom and to practice diligently.

[16] **Three Turnings of the Dharma Wheel and the Twelve Aspects of the Four Noble Truths:** *Skt. "tri-parivarta-dvadasakara-dharma-cakra-pravartana."* According to the

Connected Discourses of the Buddha, fas. 15, the teachings of "Three Turnings of the Dharma Wheel and the Twelve Aspects of the Four Noble Truths" have the characteristics of insightfully seen (*caksus*), decidedly cut off (*jnana*), studied and understood (*vidya*), and awakened (*buddhi*).

[17] *Yogacarabhumi Sastra*: Ch. "*Yuqie Shidi Lun.*" Discoursed by Maitreya Bodhisattva, recorded by Asanga, and translated into Chinese by Xuanzang (T: vol. 30, no. 1579). This commentary is the basic text for the Yogacara School and the most important teaching in the Mind-Only school. It is also known as "*the Commentary on the Seventeen Stages.*"

[18] *Commentary on the Madhyamika Sastra:* Ch. *Zhong Lun Shu* or *Zhong Lun Guan Shu*. It is the work of Chinese Master Jiaxiang Jizang in 608 C.E. (T: vol. 42, no. 1824.)

[19] **the six realms:** Indicating the six places of existence; the realms of heaven, asura, human, animal, hungry ghost and hell.

[20] **the three vehicles:** *Skt. "trini yanani."* The vehicles of the sravaka, the pratyeka-buddha, and bodhisattva.

[21] **Three Dharma Seals:** Also known as the Three Marks of Existence. According to the *Connected Discourses of the Buddha* in the *Chinese Buddhist Canon*, they are 1) All condi-

tioned dharmas are impermanent (*anityah sarva-samskarah*); 2) All dharmas are without self (*niratmanah saarva-dharmaah*); 3) Nirvana is equanimity (*santam nirvanam*). In some Buddhist texts such as in *Dhammapada*, they are 1) All compounded things are impermanent; 2) All compounded things are unsatisfied; 3) All dharmas are without self.

[22] ***Gradual Discourses of the Buddha (Ekottarikagama Sutra):*** Ch. *"Zeng Yi Ahan Jing;"* in Pali, Anguttara Nikaya. Translated into Chinese by Qutan Sengqie Tipo (*skt. Gautama Sangha Deva?*) It contains 52 fascicles and 472 sutras. Compared with other agamas, it is the last developed completely and it embraces the Mahayana philosophy. It was named such because the Buddha gradually discourses the methods of practice from one kind to eleven kinds.

[23] **eight adversities:** *Skt. "astav aksanah,"* indicating eight kinds of obstructions that prevent one from hearing or learning the Buddha's teachings. The obstructions are rebirth 1) in the realm of hell; 2) in the realm of hungry ghost; 3) in the realm of animal; 4) in the realm of Asamjnisattvah (one of heavens); 5) on the border of a Pure Land (because as one cultivated and accumulated merits and virtues, one had doubts); 6) in the realm of human, but with a disability such as being blind, deaf, or mute; 7) in the human realm, but without believing or studying Buddhism, and only studying worldly knowledge; and 8) at the time before or after the Buddha physically manifested.

[24] **the right path:** Indicating the path leading to liberation that the Buddha taught.

[25] ***Connected Discourses of the Buddha*** (*Samyuktagama Sutra*): *Ch.* "*Zhong Ahan Jing*;" in Pali "*Samyutta Nikaya.*" It was translated into Chinese by Gunabhadra (394-468 C.E.), and contains 1362 sutras in 50 fascicles (T. vol.2, no.99). It is named such because the objects the Buddha teaches includes bhiksus, bhiksunis, upaskas, upasikas, and heavenly beings, and the teachings also include several subjects such as the Four Noble Truths, Eightfold Noble Path, and Dependent Origination. There are now two English versions. One is translated by Bhikkhu Bodhi and the other is translated by El Woodward, entitled "*Kindred Sayings* Vol. I-V."

[26] **sramana:** One epithet of a monastic. Usually it is used by the monastics to refer to themselves.

[27] **brahmans:** or "*brahmins*," the highest of four castes in ancient India. Traditionally, they were teachers and interpreters of religious knowledge. They were also the priests who acted as intermediaries between gods, the world, and humans. They were the only group allowed to perform religious rituals.

[28] **bhiksus:** A Sanskrit term for the male members of the Buddhist community who have renounced the household life

and received full ordination. The female members with full ordination are called "bhiksunis." According to the *Treatise on Perfection of Great Wisdom*, literally, the word "bhiksu" can be traced back to the word "bhiks" (begging) and the word of "bhinna-klesa" (eliminating afflictions). Therefore, bhiksus/bhiksunis are also known as beggars or the ones who eliminate afflictions.

[29] **Deer Park:** *Skt. "Mrgadava,"* today known as *"Sarnath"* or *"Saranganatha."* Its location is close to the city of Varanasi in North India.

[30] *Medallion Sutra on the Bodhisattva Path*: *Ch. "Pusa Yingluo [Benye] Jing."* It was translated by Zhu Fonian in 376-378 C.E.. The main contents describe the bodhisattva stages and methods of upholding and practicing the three precepts to benefit sentient beings.

[31] *Four Part Vinaya* (*Dharmagupta Vinaya*): *Ch. "Si Fen Lu."* Originally, it was the Vinaya of the Dharmagupta School in the Theravada System (known as *"Arya-sthavira-nikaya"* in Sanskrit.). It was translated into Chinese by Zhu Fonian and Buddhayasas in 410-412 C.E. (T: vol. 30, no. 1564.)

[32] *Middle Length Discourses of the Buddha* (*Madhyamagama Sutra*): *Ch. "Zhong Ahan Jing"* (T: vol. 1, no. 26), translated into Chinese by Samghadeva; in Pali, *"Majhima Nikaya."* It is

named such because it is the collection of the sutras which are neither long nor short. Its contents include the words and deeds of Sakyamuni Buddha and his disciples, and the basic doctrines of Buddhism such as the Four Noble Truths, the Eightfold Noble Path, and Dependent Origination.

[33] **impermanence:** *Skt.* "*anitya*" or "*anityata.*" One of the most basic truths taught by the Buddha. It is the concept that all conditioned dharmas or phenomena will arise, abide, change, and disappear due to causes and conditions.

[34] **the Eightfold Noble Path:** *Skt.* "*aryastangikamaga*"; in Pali, "*ariya-atthangika-magga*". The word of "*ariya*" means noble or correct.

[35] *Chinese Buddhist Canon*: The oldest version was translated in the Chinese Han Dynasty. In that period, the representative translating Hinayana sutras was An Shigao; the representative translating Mahayana sutras was Lokasema. Until the fourth century, the categories of canons began to be classified by Daoan. After the Chinese Tang Dynasty, the Chinese Buddhist Canon became more complete due to the great efforts of many monastic scholars. It was during the Chinese Song Dynasty that it began to be printed and published by the official government. In the Chinese Qing Dynasty, there were several editions published. According to the Japanese Taisho version, "Da Zang Jing" is reprinted again. In this text, the listed categories are

based on this edition.

[36] ***Tripitaka:*** *Skt.* "*tri*" means three and "*pitaka*" refers to basket; *Ch.* "*San Zang.*" The Tripitaka is the Pali Buddhist Canon, which is comprised of three groups: Sutra, Vinaya, and Abhidharma.

[37] ***Treatise on the Middle Path*** (Mulamadhyamaka Karika): *Ch.* "*Zhong Guan Lun.*" It was written by Nagarjuna, explained by Pingala, and translated into Chinese by Kumarajiva (T: vol. 30, no. 1564).

[38] **Confucianism:** The philosophy of Confucius, whose statement stresses the principle of magnanimity (*Ch. Zhong Shu Zhi Dao*), which includes the concepts of the harmony of society through individual virtues, the development of virtues based on the fulfillment of *Jen* (*ren*), usually translated as "humanity," and the manifestation of *Jen* through the expressions of *Li*, known as politeness, good manner, and proper rituals. His famous work is called "*the Classic of Confucius*" (*Ch.* "*Lun Yu*").

[39] **four ethical principles:** Indicating propriety (*li*), justice (*yi*), honesty (*lian*), and a sense of shame (*chi*).

[40] **eight cardinal values:** Including loyalty (*zhong*), filial piety

(*xiao*), humanity (*ren*), benevolence and love (*ai*), trustfulness and faith (*xin*), righteousness (*yi*), harmony (*he*), and peace (*ping*).

[41] **three bonds in human relationships:** Indicating the relationships of emperor and minister, father and son (parents and children), and husband and wife.

[42] **five constant virtues:** Referring to a father's righteousness, mother's benevolence, elder brother/sister's love, the young's respect, and son/daughter's filial piety.

[43] **Mahayana, Theravada, and Vajrayana:** Three major schools of Buddhism. Mahayana is also known as Northern Buddhism, prevailing over East Asia (China, Japan, Korea, etc.). Theravada is also known as Southern Buddhism, spreading over South and Southeast Asia (Burma, Kampuchea, Laos, Sri Lanka, Thailand, etc.). Vajrayana is also named "Diamond Vehicle," popular in Central Asia, India , and Tibet, as well as in China and Japan.

[44] **twelve sections of the *Buddhist Canon*:** *Skt. "dvadasanga-buddha-vacana."* Thee twelve categories of the Buddh's teachings, classified by format and content. The twelve categories are: 1) *sutra* (prose); 2) *geya* (verses that correspond to the sutra); 3) *vyakaraana* (originally indicating the explanation of teachings, later referring to the Buddha's prophecy to his disci-

ples); 4) *gatha* (verse only); 5) *udana* (the Buddha discourses the Dharma, without waiting for someone to make this request); 6) *nidana* (describing the causes and conditions of the Buddha's discoursing); 7) *avadana* (parables); 8) *itivrttaka* (describing the stories of the previous lives of the Buddha and his disciples); 9) *jataka* (describing the Buddha's practices of great compassion in his previous lives); 10) *vaipula* (instructing the profound teachings); 11) *adbhuta-dharma* (describing the special events of the Buddha and his disciples); 12) *upadesa* (describing the Buddha's interpretation about the nature of all dharmas and meanings).

[45] **King Ajatasatru:** The son of King Bimbisara of the Magadha Kingdom in ancient India. He killed his father and usurped his throne. Later, he became one of the Buddha's disciples.

[46] **the five vehicles:** Indicates the vehicles of human (*manusya-yana*), heaven (deva-yana), sravaka, pratyeka-buddha, and bodhisattva.

[47] **the five bhiksus:** Refers to the first five monks: Kaundinya, Asvajit, Bhadrika, Dasabala-Kasyapa and Mahanama. Originally, they were the attendants of Prince Siddharttha (Sakyamuni Buddha) and followed the prince when he left the palace. After his enlightenment, the Buddha discoursed the Four Noble Truths to them and they became his disciples. This was the beginning of the Sangha establishment.

[48] **the sravakas and the pratyeka-buddhas:** Literally, the word "sravaka" means hearer, and it refers to one who has attained enlightenment after listening to the Buddha's teachings. "pratyeka-buddha" refers to those who awaken to the Truth through their own efforts when they live in the time without a Buddha's presence.

[49] **the Small Vehicle:** *Skt.* "*Hinayana.*" Literally, it means that the Vehicle can only carry a few people to liberation, from the Mahayana interpretation. It indicates one who only focuses on self cultivation.

[50] ***Lion's Roar of Queen Srimala Sutra*** (*Srimala devismhanada Sutra*): *Ch. "Shengman Jing.*" Translated by Gunabhadra (394 ~ 468); (T: vol. 12, no. 353). This sutra is expounded by King Prasenajit's daughter of Sravasti (Srimala). The main points in this sutra are the concept of one vehicle, the noble truths, dharmakaya, and the Buddha Nature. It also describes Srimala making ten promises and three great vows in front of the Buddha. This sutra is one of the representative sutras expounded by the layperson, like the *Vimalakirti Sutra*; it is also an authoritative text that a woman can become a Buddha.

[51] ***Great Nirvana Sutra*** (*Mahaparinirvana Sutra*): There are three versions in the *Chinese Buddhist Canon*. One version was translated by Faxian, called "*Fo Shuo Dabo Nihuan Jing,*" with six fascicles (T: vol. 12, no. 376.). Another was translated by

Dharmaraksa, named "*Dabo Niepan Jing*," with 40 fascicles (T: vol. 12, no. 374). The other is also named such, but some contents were added and revised by Master Huiyan in the Chinese Song Dynasty. In total this version includes 36 fascicles (T: vol. 12, no. 375).

[52] **the five aggregates:** *Skt.* "*skandhas*" means aggregates; and the five aggregates are form, feeling, perception, mental formations, and consciousness.

[53] **the Law of Cause and Effect:** *Skt.* "*hetu-phala*." This is the most basic doctrine in Buddhism, which explains the formation of all relations and connections in the world. This law means that the arising of each and every phenomenon is due to its own causes and conditions, and the actual form, or appearance, of all phenomena is the effect.

[54] *Abhidharmamahavibhasa Sastra***:** *Ch.* "*Apidamo Dapiposha Lun*," translated into Chinese by Xuanzang (T: vol. 27, no. 1545). This commentary is the explanation and interpretation of *Abhidharma-jnana-prasthana Sastra*, which is the work of Katyayaniputra. Traced back to Buddhist history, this commentary was compiled by King Kaniska of the Kusana Kingdom and the Elder Parsva with five hundred arhats in the Fourth Council. The major contents are associated with the interpretations of the Sarvastivadin philosophy.

⁵⁵ *Mahayanabhidharma Samuccaya Vyakhya*: Ch. *"Dasheng Apidamo Za Ji Lun."* This contains the original text and the explanations of *Mahayanabhidharma Samuccaya* written by Asangha, edited by Sthirabodhih, and translated into Chinese by Xuanzang (T: vol. 31, no. 1606). It is an important text of the Mind-Only School.

⁵⁶ *Treatise on Demonstration of Mind-Only* (*Vijnaptimatratasiddhi Sastra*): Also known as the *Demonstration of Consciousness Only* (BDK Publications). *Ch. "Cheng Weishi Lun."* It is the explanation of Vasubhandu's the *Thirty Verses on Mind Only*. This work was done by Dharmapala and nine other great commentators in 557 C.E., then it was translated into Chinese by Xuanzang (T: vol. 31, no. 1585).

⁵⁷ *Explanation of the Mahayana*: Ch. *"Dasheng Yi Zhang."* (T: vol. 44, no. 1851). It is the work of Huiyuan (523-592 C.E.). The main statements in this book are about the philosophy and doctrines of Mahayana Buddhism.

⁵⁸ *Great Commentary on the Flower Ornament Sutra*: Ch. *"Huayan Da Shu* or *Da Fang Guang Fo Huayan Jing Shu."* It is the work of Master Chengguan, completed in 783-784 C.E. The main contents are the explanations and interpretations of the main points of the 80 fascicles in the *Flower Ornament Sutra* (T. vol.35, no.1735).

[59] **dharmakaya:** The body of Dharma, which indicates the true nature of the Buddha or the unity of Buddha with all phenomena.

[60] **samadhi:** Literally, "establish, or make firm." It means meditative concentration; a state in which the mind is concentrated on one-pointed focus and all mental activities are calm. In samadhi, one is free from all distractions, thereby entering a state of inner serenity.

[61] **the five contemplations:** Five methods of contemplation for stopping and eliminating delusions: 1) Contemplation on the impurity of the body (*Skt. asubha-smrti*). This enables sentient beings to eliminate greed in the mind. 2) Contemplation on compassion (*Skt. maritri-smrti*). This enables sentient beings to eliminate anger and hatred in the mind. 3) Contemplation on Dependent Origination (*Skt. idampratyayata-pratiyasamutpada-smrti*). This enables sentient beings to eliminate ignorance and afflictions in the mind. 4) Contemplation on a Buddha's name (*Skt. buddhanusmrti*). This enables sentient beings to eliminate unwholesome thoughts and the stress of uncomfortable situations. Sometimes this method is replaced by "Contemplation on the worlds" (*Skt. dhatu-prabheda-smrti*), also known as contemplation on analysis or non-self, which is based on the concept that all phenomena are made up of the elements of earth, fire, water, wind, consciousness, and emptiness. This form of contemplation helps sentient beings to eliminate their attachment to

self. 5) Contemplation on breathing (*Skt. anapana-smrti*). This helps sentient beings to eliminate distracted states of mind and achieve one-pointedness of mind.

[62] the six wondrous ways to nirvana: The six methods of meditation in the Tiantai School. 1) The first method is to count breathing from one to ten (*shu xi men*), making the mind enter meditative concentration. 2) The second method is to follow breathing without counting (*sui xi men*). It is the second stage in which the mind naturally concentrates on breathing therefore counting is not necessary. 3) The method of stopping [delusion] (*zhi men*) is the third, which helps individuals to eliminate delusions and then stay in the state of samadhi naturally. 4) The method of seeing [truth] (*guan men*) is the way to help individuals be insightful to five aggregates due to causes and conditions, then help individuals eliminate the wrong views, and finally help individuals have true wisdom in the mind. 5) The method of returning [to the original mind] (*huan men*), in which attachment to self has been eliminated. 6) The method of purity (*jing men*), in which the mind has no more attachment, only purity and true wisdom. The first three belong to the category of concentration; the latter three belong to the category of wisdom.

[63] the nine stages of meditative concentration: The methods for meditating practitioners to concentrate on one-pointedness of mind. 1) The stage of stability (*anzhu xin*); 2) The stage of embracing (*shezhu xin*); 3) The stage of discriminated perception (*jiezhu xin*); 4) The stage of stopping perception and returning to the original mind (*zhuanzhu xin*); 5) The stage of taming (*fuzhu xin*); 6) The stage of stopping thoughts (*xizhu xin*); 7) The stage of eliminating greed and craving (*miezhu xin*); 8) The stage of understanding original nature (*xingzhu xin*); 9) The stage of continually attending samadhi (*chizhu xin*).

[64] ***Flower Ornament Sutra*** (*Avatamsaka Sutra*): Ch. *Huayan (Hua-Yen) Jing*; in Sanskrit, its whole title is "*Buddhavatamsaka Mahavaipula Sutra*." It is one of the most important sutras in the Mahayana school. There are three different versions (T: vol. 9, no. 278, no. 279 & no. 293) in the *Chinese Buddhist Canon*. They are 1) 60 fascicles, translated by Buddhabhadra (359-429); 2) 80 fascicles, translated by Siksananda (652-710); 3) 40 fascicles, translated by Prajna (734-?).

[65] **the Saha World:** Literally, "saha" means endurance. It indicates the present world where we reside, which is full of suffering to be endured. The beings in this world endure suffering and afflictions due to their greed, anger, hatred, and ignorance.

[66] ***Collection of Great Treasures*** (*Maharatnakuta*): Ch. *Da Baoji Jing*. The title refers to the accumulation of great Dharma treasures and innumerable methods. The major content is related to the bodhisattvas' cultivation methods and the predicting records of their progress in attaining Buddhahood. The methods include the teachings and practices of emptiness, and the Pure

Land and Esoteric schools.

⁶⁷ *Treatise on the Four Noble Truths* (*Catuhsatya-nirdesha*): Ch. "*Si Di Lun.*" It is the work of Vasuvarman and was translated into Chinese by Zhendi (T: vol. 32, no. 1647).

⁶⁸ three realms: Indicating the realms of the sense-desires (*kama-dhatu*), form (*rupa-dhatu*), and formlessness (*arupa-dhatu*), where sentient beings transmigrate in the cycle of birth and death.

⁶⁹ Early Buddhism: Titled for the specific period of Buddhism, from the time when Sakyamuni Buddha established the Sangha to 100-200 years after his parinirvana. In that period, the Buddhism in India had not divided into eighteen schools yet.

⁷⁰ the power of our vows: Please see endnote no. 7 (way of vowing).

⁷¹ the power of other's vows: This refers to the power of the great vows of the highly cultivated masters, bodhisattvas, or Buddhas; for example, Amitabha Buddha made forty-eight great vows, and because of them sentient beings can be reborn in the Western Pure Land where they can cultivate themselves under better conditions.

[72] *Treatise on Perfection of the Great Wisdom* (*Mahaprajnaparamita Sastra*): Ch. "Da Zhidu Lun." It is the commentary on the *Sutra on the Perfection of Great Wisdom*, written by Nagarjuna and translated into Chinese by Kumarajiva in 402-405 C.E. (T: vol. 25, no. 1509), one of the four great translators in Chinese Buddhist history. This treatise contains detailed interpretations of Buddhist doctrines, philosophies, legends, history, geography, and rules of practice and the Sangha. The main subjects are the philosophy and spirit of the bodhisattva in Mahayana Buddhism, and the practices of the six perfections.

[73] **the worldly path:** Refers to chanting a Buddha's name as a method of being reborn in his Pure Land.

[74] **the transcendental path:** Refers to cultivating the ten thousand practices and six perfections in the saha world as a means of achieving enlightenment.

[75] **the path of five vehicles or the path of Mahayana:** The path of five vehicles refers to the path of human, heaven, sravaka, pratyeka-buddha, and bodhisattva. The path of Mahayana refers to the "Buddha-yana" (the path to Buddhahood).

[76] **the thirty-seven practices to enlightenment** (*bodhipaksika*): The 26, 27, and 28 fascicles of the *Connected Discourses of the Buddha* contain the detailed descriptions and explanations of

these practices. Or the Chapter 16 of the *Large Sutra on Perfect Wisdom*, translated by Edward Conze.

[77] **four applications of mindfulness** (*satipatthana*): They are mindfulness on the body, feelings, thoughts and dharmas: 1) To contemplate that the body is impure; 2) To contemplate that feelings result in sufferings; 3) To contemplate that thoughts are impermanent, always arising then extinguishing; 4) To contemplate that all dharmas are due to causes and conditions based on the Law of Dependent Origination.

[78] **four right efforts** (*samyak-prahana*): 1) To eliminate unwholesomeness which has already been produced; 2) To not produce unwholesomeness which has not been produced; 3) To generate the wholesomeness which has not yet been generated; 4) To increase wholesomeness which has already been produced.

[79] **four bases of spiritual power** (*riddhipada*): 1) The spiritual power of desire-to-do, which means that all Dharmas of cultivation can be fulfilled; 2) The spiritual power of diligence, which means that the mind can concentrate on cultivation without interruptions; 3) The spiritual power of remembering, which means that the mind does not forget; 4) The spiritual power of contemplation, which means the mind contemplates all dharmas.

[80] **five faculties** (*indriya*): 1) Faith on the right path; 2) Diligence on the right dharmas; 3) Remembering the right dharmas without forgetting; 4) Concentration, in which the mind is stable and without distractions; 5) Wisdom, to contemplate and see the nature of all dharmas.

[81] **five powers** (*bala*): 1) When the power of faith increases, doubts can be eliminated. 2) When the power of diligence increases, the sloth of body and mind can be eliminated. 3) When the power of remembrance increases, unwholesome thoughts can be eliminated. 4) When the power of concentration increases, distractions can be eliminated and the state of samadhi can be attended. 5) When the power of wisdom increases, delusions can be stopped and eliminated.

[82] **seven limbs of enlightenment** (*sapta-boddhyangani*): Refers to seven kinds of practices to develop enlightenment. They are: 1) mindfulness; fully understanding and frequently staying in samadhi and possessing wisdom; 2) investigation of dharmas; discerning the true teachings based on wisdom, and abandoning the false; 3) diligence; diligently practicing the correct teachings or without sloth; 4) joyfulness; feeling joy as a result of having learnt the correct teachings; 5) ease of body and mind; the physical body and mind feel restful, peaceful, and secure; 6) concentration; attaining samadhi without distraction; 7) equanimity; without bias, clinging, or grasping, and keeping equality, equanimity, and tranquility in the mind.

[83] **Four Means of Embracing** (*catvari-samgraha-vastuni*): Four methods that bodhisattvas use to guide sentient beings to the path of liberation. They are: 1) giving (*dana-samgraha*); 2) kind words (*priya-vadita-samgraha*); 3) altruism and beneficence (*artha-carya-samgraha*); 4) sympathy and empathy (*samanarthata-samgraha*).

[84] **Master Xingan:** The Ninth Patriarch of the Pure Land School, born in the Chinese Qing Dynasty, also known as "Shixian."

[85] *Inspiration for the Bodhicitta Pledge*: Ch. "*Quan Fa Putixin Wen.*" The work of Master Xingan.

[86] **Amitabha Buddha:** The Buddha of the Western Pure Land, also known as the Buddha of Infinite Life or the Buddha of Infinite Light.

[87] *Larger Sutra on Amitayus* [*Sukhavativyuha*]: Ch. "*Wu Liang Shou Jing.*" Translated into Chinese by Samaghavarman (T: vol. 12, no. 360). It is one of three basic texts of the Pure Land School. The other two are the *Sutra on Contemplation Amitayus* and the *Smaller Sutra on Amitayus*.

[88] *Karunapundarika Sutra*: Ch. "*Bei Hua Jing.*" Translated into Chinese by Dharmaraksa (T: vol. 3, no. 157). It compares

and describes two concepts. One is to attain enlightenment in the Pure Lands, such as the Western Pure Land; the other is to achieve Buddhahood in the saha world such as Sakyamuni Buddha did. This sutra also praises the great compassion of Sakyamuni Buddha.

[89] **Maitreya Bodhisattva:** He is easily recognized and well known for his smiling and loving-kindness. According to the sutras, Maitreya Bodhisattva is presently discoursing the Dharma to the heavenly beings in Tusita Heaven.

[90] *Sutra of the Questions Asked by Maitreya*: Ch. *"Fo Shuo Mile Pusa Suowen Benyuan Jing."* Translated into Chinese by Dharmakarasa in 303 C.E..

[91] **Bhaisajyaguru Buddha** (Medicine Buddha): Literally, the word "*bhaisajya*" means medicine; "*guru*" refers to the master or teacher. Also known as the Buddha of Healing. In previous lives, when he practiced the bodhisattva path, he made twelve great vows to help sentient beings eliminate the suffering of physical and mental illness and to guide them towards liberation. Usually, when the Medicine Buddha is depicted, his left hand holds the medicine bowl and his right hand is in the gesture of protection.

[92] **the Pure Land of Azure Radiance:** Also known as the Land of Pure Crystal. The name implies that this Pure Land has the

qualities of clarity and radiance, such as the precious azure gem.

[93] ***Sutra of Medicine Buddha***: Skt. *"Bhagavan-bhaisajyaguru-vaiduryaprabhasya purvapranidhana-visesa-vistara"*; Ch. *"Yiao Shi Liuli Guang Rulai Benyuan Jing."* The most popular version was translated into Chinese by Xuanzang in 650 C.E. (T: vol. 14, no. 450). In addition to this version, there are two other translations in the *Chinese Buddhist Canon*. One was translated by Dharmagupta in 615 C.E. (T: vol. 14, no. 449); the other was translated by Yijing in 707 C.E. (T: vol. 14, no. 451).

[94] **Manjusri Bodhisattva:** *Ch. "Wenshu."* The Bodhisattva of Wisdom; he has the wisdom to see the true nature of all dharmas. He represents transcendental wisdom and is typically depicted sitting on a lion. He and Samantabhadra Bodhisattva are usually described as standing on the right and left hand side of Sakyamuni Buddha.

[95] **Samantabhadra Bodhisattva:** *Ch. "Puxian."* He personifies transcendental practice and vows. He typically sits on a white elephant with six tusks (symbolizing the six perfections). To read about his ten great vows, please see the last section of the *Flower Ornament Sutra* that contains forty fascicles (T: vol. 10, no. 293, fas. 40).

[96] **Avalokitesvara Bodhisattva:** The Bodhisattva of Compassion who can manifest in any conceivable form to bring

help to those in need. In China, Avalokitesvara is usually portrayed in the female form, known as "Kuan Yin" (*Guanyin*). For a more detailed description of the great compassion and vows of Avalokitesvara, please see the twenty-fifth chapter, Chapter of Universal Gate, in the *Lotus Sutra*.

[97] ***Lotus Sutra*** [*Saddharmapundarika Sutra*]: *Ch.: Miao Fa Lianhua Jing* or *Fahua Jing*. "*Saddharma*" in Sanskrit means good Dharma or true justice. "*Pundarika*" refers to a white lotus flower, which symbolizes that which is pure and undefiled. The whole title means that the nature of Dharma is as pure and undefiled as the white lotus flower. In the Chinese Buddhist Canon, there are three versions: 1) Translated by Zhu Fahu in 286; named *Zheng Fahua Jing* (T: vol. 9, no. 263); with 10 fascicles, 27 chapters. 2) Translated by Kumarajiva in 406; named *Miao Fa Lianhua Jing* (T: vol. 9, no. 26); with 8 fascicles, 28 chapters. This version is the easiest to understand, but most popular. This one is also the original Chinese version for most English translations. 3) Translated by Jnanagupta and Dharmagupta; named *Tian Pin Miao Fa Lianhua Jing* (T: vol. 9, no. 27); with 8 fascicles, 27 chapters. It is one of the most important sutras in Mahayana Buddhism and its major emphasis is on the concept of "*triyanas* in one." "*Triyanas*" means three vehicles, indicating the vehicles of sravakas, pretyeka-buddhas, and bodhisattvas; "*triyanas* in one" means the above three vehicles should ultimately return to One Vehicle (*Buddhayana*). The sutra also offers the message that all sentient beings are able to

attain Buddhahood. It is also a wonderful work of great literary merit, containing many sections of verse and various parables.

[98] **Ksitigarbha Bodhisattva:** Also known as the Earth Store or Earth Treasure Bodhisattva. He was entrusted by Sakyamuni Buddha to help all sentient beings in the period without the Buddhas' physical presence, between the time after Sakyamuni Buddha's parinirvana and when Maitreya Bodhisattva comes to this world to achieve Buddhahood.

[99] *Sutra on the Past Vows of the Earth Store Bodhisattva* [*Ksitigarbhapranidhana Sutra*]: *Ch. Dizang Pusa benyuan Jing*." Translated into Chinese by Siksananda (652-710 C.E.), T: vol.13, no.412. This sutra is divided into 13 chapters and the contents describe the great vows, merits, and virtues of Ksitigarbha Bodhisattva.

[100] **Tathagatas:** Literally, the word "tathagata" is translated as Thus-Come One, meaning one who has attained full realization of suchness; i.e. become one with the absolute, so that he can go anywhere he wants. It is also one of the ten epithets of the Buddha. Here, "Tathagatas" refers to all Buddhas.

[101] *Sixth Patriarch Platform Sutra*: *Ch. "Liu Zu Tan Jing."* Discoursed by Master Huineng, recorded by his disciple, Fahai, in the Tang Dynasty, and later edited by Zongbao in the Chinese Yuan Dynasty. This sutra is divided into ten chapters and is an

important text in the Chan School.

[102] *Sutra on the Practice of Prajnaparamita*: *Ch. "Daoxing Bore Jing."* Translated into Chinese by Lokasema in 179 C.E. (T: vol. 8, no. 224). In the *Chinese Buddhist Canon*, this sutra is the oldest translated version in the series of prajna-wisdom sutras. It describes the teachings and methods of prajnaparamita (the perfection of wisdom), and also mentions what kinds of merits and virtues will be gained after practicing.

[103] *Collection of Dharanis*: *Ch. "Tuoluoni Za Ji."* The author is unknown. It contains dharanis from various sutras and describes the merits and virtues that will be gained after reciting them.

[104] *Great Techniques of Stopping [Delusion] and Seeing [Truth]*: *Ch. "Mohe Zhi Guan,"* (T. vol.46, no.1911). This work was instructed by Master Zhiyi, and recorded by his disciple, Guanding, in 594 C.E. The content describes the meditation methods of *Zhi* (stopping) and *Guan* (seeing), as well as Master Zhiyi's personal meditation experiences.

[105] *Ceremonial Procedures for Transmission of the Bodhicitta Precepts*: *Ch. "Shuo Puti Xin Jie Yi."* Translated into Chinese by Amoghavajra (T. vol.18, no.915). It is the text for the disciples receiving the Dharma transmission to take the bodhicitta precepts in the Tantric School.

[106] **the Japanese Tendai School:** Japanese form of the Chinese Tiantai (Tientai) School; brought to Japan in the eighth century by Master Zuicheng (in Chinese).

[107] *Surangama Sutra*: *Ch. "Da Fo Dingshou Lengyan Jing."* Translated into Chinese by Pramiti in 705 C.E. (T: vol. 19, no. 945). It is a very important text for meditation practitioners. The methods of meditative concentration and the bodhisattva path are both discussed in this sutra.

[108] *Glossary of Translated Terms*: The work of Fayun in the Chinese Song Dynasty (T: vol. 53, no. 2131); the Chinese-Sanskrit dictionary, including 2040 Buddhist terms classified in 64 chapters.

[109] *The Way to Buddhahood*: *Ch. "Cheng Fo Zhi Dao."* It is the work of Venerable Yin-shun and was translated by Dr. Wing H. Yeung and published by Wisdom Publications in 1998. To read about the three principles of a bodhisattva mentioned in this context, please see pages 219-221.

[110] *Diamond Sutra* [*Vajracchedika Prajnaparamita Sutra*]: *Ch. "Jingang Jing."* There are several versions, translated into Chinese by Kumarajiva, Bodhiruci, and Zhendi (T: vol. 8, no. 235, 236 & 237). "*Vajracchedika*" means the diamond that cuts through afflictions, ignorance, delusions, or illusions; "*prajna-*

paramita" is the perfection of wisdom, and it brings sentient beings across the sea of suffering to the other shore. (Reference from *The Diamond That Cuts Through Illusion* by Thich Nhat Han).

[111] **suchness:** *Skt. "tathata,"* a term for the true nature of all things; the pure, original essence of all phenomena.

[112] **accessory afflictions:** *Skt. "upaklesa."* Afflictions that arise from the roots of afflictions. According to the Treatise on Demonstration of Mind-Only, there are three kinds: 1) minor accessory afflictions, including "anger, hostility, dissmulation, vexation, envy, avarice, deceit, hypocrisy, with harmfulness and vanity"; 2) middle accessory afflictions, no sense of shame and conscience; 3) primary aceessory afflictions, "agitation, torpor, unbelief, indolence, negligence, forgetfulness, distraction, and incorrect knowing." (English reference from *Three Texts`on Consciousness Only*, page 379).

[113] **five *vidyas*:** In traditional system of education in ancient India, these are the five required courses of study. Please see *Studies in the Buddhist Culture of India*, p.127-128.

[114] **six sense organs:** Eye, ear, nose, tongue, body, and mind.

[115] **eight consciousness** [*astau vijnanani*]: The consciousness of

eye, ear, nose, tongue, body, mind (*mano-vijnana*, which is the consciousness of discrimination), *manas* (the consciousness of attachment to self), and *alaya* (the store consciousness).

[116] **three great *kalpas*:** The word "*kalpa*" is the measuring unit of time in ancient India; a kalpa is an immense and inconceivable length of time. Buddhism adapts it to refer the period of time between the creation and recreation of the worlds. A great kalpa in Sanskrit is "*asamkhyeya-kalpa*," and the word "*asamkya*" means innumerable. According to the sutras, bodhisattvas need to spend three great kalpas in cultivating ten thousand practices and six perfections to accumulate merits and virtues.

[117] **a hundred *kalpas*:** After three-great-*kalpas* of cultivation, bodhisattvas need to spend one hundred kalpas in cultivation to reach the level of "equal enlightenment" in bodhisattva path (the fifty-first in the fifty-two levels of the bodhisattva path).

[118] **the supreme marks:** The thirty-two excellent marks of the Buddha and the eighty accessory marks.

[119] **the Buddha:** Here, it refers to the Mahabhijna-jnanabhibhu Tathagata, translated as "Great Universal Wisdom Excellence Buddha."

[120] **maras:** A Sanskrit term, literally translated as evils or devils. In Buddhism, it is defined as the one who hinders the practitioner in doing goodness or seeking liberation. While the Buddha was seeking liberation, maras frequently appeared as obstructions to impede his enlightenment.

[121] **Master Zhiyi:** The founder of the Tiantai (Tientai) School in Chinese Buddhism (538-597); also known as the Great Master of Zhizhe (the Wise) or Tiantai. His many works include *Great Techniques of Stopping [Delusion] and Seeing [Truth]*, *Profound Meanings of Lotus Sutra (Fahua Jing Xuan Yi)*, and *Explanations on the Passages and Sentences of Lotus Sutra (Fahua Wen Ju)*. Together, these three are known as "the three great works of the Tiantai School."

[122] ***Bodhisattva Medallion Sutra*:** Ch. *"Pusa Yingluo Jing,"* translated into Chinese by Zhu Fonian (T: vol. 16, no. 656); contains fourteen fascicles.

[123] **World Honored One:** One of the ten epithets of the Buddha. Traced back to the original Sanskrit term, "*loka-natha*" refers to the lord of the worlds, or "*loka-jyestha*" means the most venerable of the world. Today, it is usually translated as "World-Honored One."

[124] **the *Agama Sutras*:** Also known as the *Nikayas* in the Pali

Canon, it includes the *Long Discourses*, the *Middle Length Discourses*, the *Connected Discourses*, and the *Gradual Discourses of the Buddha*. The contents of the *Agamas* and the *Nikayas* are slightly different due to the different original versions among the early Indian schools.

[125] ***Long Discourses of the Buddha*** (*Dirghagama*): Ch. *"Chang Ahan Jing;"* in Pali, *Digha Nikaya*. Translated into Chinese by Buddhayasas and Zhu Fonian in 413 C.E (T: vol. 1, no. 1). The version is composed of thirty sutras in four parts. The Pali version includes thirty-four sutras in three parts. The content varies slightly between the two versions due to interpretations and translations that sought to emphasize different schools of Buddhism.

[126] **I and others:** Sakyamuni Buddha and his disciples.

[127] **eight precepts:** The eight precepts of purification: 1) no killing; 2) no stealing; 3) no sexual conduct; 4) no lying; 5) no take drugs or intoxicants; 6) no sleeping on the adorned and broad bed; 7) no singing, dancing, and putting on adornment; 8) no eating during non-regulated time. They are for laity to experience one day-and-night of monastic life.

[128] **believers in brahmana:** In this context, "*brahmana*" is different from the traditional definition. Here, it indicates those who practice the path of purification or the path leading to liber-

ation.

[129] **go to the numerous gardens:** Refers to going to the Dharma assemblies. During the Buddha's time, many kings or elders offered their gardens to the Buddha for discoursing the Dharma.

[130] **Contemplating on the Enlightened One and his tender golden body:** The Enlightened One refers to the Buddha, and this term is one of the ten epithets of the Buddha. "Tender golden body" is classified into two characteristics, the softness of body and the golden-hued body, which are two of the thirty-two excellent marks of the Buddha.

[131] **the wanderers:** Sentient beings transmigrating in the sea of birth and death.

[132] **the *Atthakavagga*:** The name of one category of sutras in Pali Canon, indicating that the *Cula Niddesa* belonged to the *Sutta Nipata*.

[133] **outflows** (*asrava*): Ch. "*you lou,*" literally, "*lou*" means leaking. In Buddhism, it is one epithet of afflictions.

[134] **the state of without outflows** (*anasrava*): Ch. "*wu lou.*" Refers to the state of liberation. Sometimes "without outflows,"

refers to those dharmas free from afflictions and leading to liberation.

[135] **the liberation of mind:** *Skt. "citta-vimukti."* The mind that is liberated from craving, grasping, clinging and desires through the practice of samadhi (meditative concentration), in which one's mind has entirely eliminated greed, root cause for the above.

[136] **the liberation of wisdom:** *Skt. "prajna-vimukti."* The mind that is liberated from afflictions through prajna-wisdom, in which one's mind has eliminated ignorance.

[137] **upasaka:** A layman; a male follower of Buddhism who does not renounce the household life and enter a monastery but who still strives to live a spiritually cultivated life and uphold the teachings and precepts. Female: "upasika."

[138] **the sixteen states of practice:** They are: 1) having faith; 2) upholding the precepts of purification; 3) practicing giving; 4) going to see and visit the monastics; 5) studying the Dharma; 6) practicing the Dharma; 7) contemplating the Dharma; 8) fully understanding and cultivating the Dharma step by step. The other eight are to encourage and help others establish and practice the first eight.

[139] **the eleven states of practice:** They are to understand 1) that all phenomena are made up of four elements (earth, water, fire, and wind); 2) how to establish and increase the wisdom; 3) how to eliminate the arising of desire and hatred; 4) how to protect the six sense organs; 5) how to instruct and explain the Dharma to others; 6) the Eightfold Noble Path 7) to feel joyfulness while practicing the path to liberation; 8) how to go to the Dharma assemblies and ask for the teachings-what is right or wrong, what should or should not be done; 9) the four applications of mindfulness and the way of saints and sages (the right path); 10) how to properly accept offerings from others; 11) how to respect the virtuous monastics and learn the teachings from them.

[140] **the Four Immeasurable States of Mind:** *Skt. "catvary apramanani."* 1) The state of boundless loving-kindness (*maitry-apramana*); to give others happiness; 2) The state of boundless compassion (*karunapramana*); to help others away from suffering; 3) The state of boundless joy (*muditapramana*); to feel joyful as others can stay away from sufferings; 4) The sate of boundless equanimity (*upeksapramana*); to treat others equally without discrimination.

[141] **Blessed One** (*Bhagavan*): Or "*Bhagavat;*" *Ch.* "*Zhongyou*" in the early translations; "*Shizun*" in the latter translated works. Usually it is translated "World Honored One" in English.

[142] **the honored one:** The Buddha's disciple, Sariputra, who was

known as the foremost in wisdom.

[143] **the secondary and tertiary disciples:** Secondary disciples are those who have been monastics for 10-19 years. Tertiary disciples are those who have been monastics for 0-9 years. The other definition is based on one's virtues and cultivation of Dharma.

[144] **the ten contemplations:** They are to contemplate: 1) the Buddha; 2) the Dharma; 3) the Sangha; 4) precepts; 5) giving; 6) celestial beings; 7) stopping and seeing (*Zhi Guan*); 8) breathing; 9) the body 10) death.

[145] **the ten unwholesome conducts:** They are: 1) killing; 2) stealing; 3) sexual misconduct; 4) lying; 5) duplicity; 6) harsh words; 7) flattery; 8) greed; 9) hatred; and 10) ignorance.

[146] **the ten wholesome conducts:** The ten actions are the opposite of the above ten unwholesome deeds.

[147] **the seven techniques to understand the Dharma:** In addition to the three mentioned in this paper, the other four are to diligently learn the Dharma, to have effort, to have right thought, and to diligently practice meditation.

[148] **Bhiksus of unconditioned dharma:** In Sanskrit, uncondi-

tioned dharma is "*asamskrta dharma*;" it is apart from arising, abiding, changing and extinguishing. It is one of epithet for nirvana. In this context, it refers to the bhiksus who have already eliminated all afflictions.

[149] **the state without remainders** (*niravasesa*): The state in which afflictions and the physical body have both been extinguished.

[150] **the fruit of sramana:** The word "*sramana*" means cultivation, purification, as well as stopping and eliminating unwholesomeness. The fruit of sramana indicates the effect that results from practice.

[151] **Ananda:** One of the ten great disciples of the Buddha. He is noted as the foremost in hearing and learning. After the Buddha entered parinirvana, Ananda is said to have compiled the sutras in Vaibhara Cave, which is in Magadha, India, and which is where the five hundred disciples of the Buddha were assembled.

[152] **the heavenly realm:** *Skt.* "*deva-loka.*" The realms above the human world, including the six heavens in the realm of sense-desires, the sixteen or seventeen heavens in the realm of form, and the four heavens in the realm of formlessness.

[153] **the lower realms:** The realms of animal, hungry ghost, and

hell.

[154] **causes and conditions:** *Skt.* "*hetu-pratyaya.*" "*Hetu*" means the cause, which refers to the direct reason for a particular effect. *Hetu* is also known as the inner cause or the primary cause. "*Pratyaya*" is translated as condition, which refers to the indirect causes resulting from external circumambience, also known as the secondary cause or the external cause.

[155] **the dominant condition:** Conditions are divided into four kinds; *hetu-pratyaya, samanantara-pratyaya, alambaana-pratyaya*, and *adhipati-pratyaya*. The dominant condition is the fourth. And it is the strengthening and stimulating indirect cause between the arising and effect of all phenomena.

[156] **Bhiksu Purna:** In Pali, "*Punna,*" one of the ten great disciples of the Buddha and known as the foremost in preaching the Dharma.

[157] **Syamaka Bodhisattva:** One of Sakyamuni Buddha's previous lives during which he practiced the bodhisattva path. To read this story, please see the Chapter of Syamaka Bodhisattva in the *Sutra on the Practices of Six Perfections* (*Liu Du Ji Jing*, T. vol.3, fas.5, ch.43).

[158] **Chan Master Guishan Lingyou:** The founder of Guiyang

sect (771-853). He was the student and the chief disciple of Baizhang Huaihai. His work is called "*Sayings of Chan Master Guishan Lingyou.*"

[159] **Chan Master Zhishun:** A Chan master in the Chinese Tang Dynasty.

[160] **Prince Sudana:** He was one of the previous lives of Sakyamuni Buddha, and he also was well known in practicing the perfection of giving. To learn more about him, please see the Chapter of Sudana, the *Sutra on Practices of the Six Perfections* (T. vol.3, p7-11).

[161] **Chan Master Baiyin:** In Chinese, his name is known as "Baiyin Huihe" (1685-1768 C.E.). He was a Chan Master of the Japanese Rinzai School. Usually, he is called the Father of the Modern Rinzai School in Japan.

[162] **Chan Master Baizhang:** Also known as "*Baizhang Huaihai.*" He studied with Chan Master Mazu Daoyi and established the system in which the Sangha provides its own daily necessities by cultivating vegetables. This kind of system is called "the monastic regulations of Baizhang (*Ch. Baizhang Qing Gui*). His work is known as "*Sayings of Chan Master Baizhang.*"

[163] **Master Xuanzang:** A great master in the Chinese Tang Dynasty (602? - 664 C.E.). He was one of four great translators in Chinese Buddhist history. He studied in India for seventeen years and was an expert of the *Tripitaka*. His famous work is called "*Buddhist Records of the Western Regions*" (*Da Tang Xiyu Ji*).

[164] **Master Taixu:** Usually known as "Tai-hsu" (1889-1947 C.E.). He is the reformer of Chinese Buddhism in the late nineteenth and early twentieth century. His works are included in the set of the *Complete Works of Taixu* (*Taixu Dashi Quan Shu*).